GU00891340

PARLIAMENTS AND GOVERNMENTS IN THE NEXT MILLENNIUM

Cavendish
Publishing
Limited

London • Sydney

PARLIAMENTS AND GOVERNMENTS IN THE NEXT MILLENNIUM

Written and compiled by

Priyanee Wijesekera
Deputy Secretary General of the
Parliament of Sri Lanka

and

Diana Reynolds
Assistant Director of Development and
Planning in the CPA Secretariat

Cavendish
Publishing
Limited

London • Sydney

First published in Great Britain 1999 by Cavendish Publishing Limited,
The Glass House, Wharton Street, London WC1X 9PX, United Kingdom
Telephone: + 44 (0) 20 7278 8000   Facsimile: + 44 (0) 20 7278 8080
E-mail: info@cavendishpublishing.com
Visit our Home Page on http://www.cavendishpublishing.com

© The Commonwealth Parliamentary Association   1999

No part of this publication may be reproduced, stored in a retrieval system, or
transmitted in any form or by any means, electronic, mechanical,
photocopying, recording or otherwise, without the prior permission of the
publisher and copyright owner.

Any person who infringes the above in relation to this publication may be
liable to criminal prosecution and civil claims for damages.

Cataloguing in Publication Data

Parliaments and governments in the next millennium
1. Legislative bodies 2. Legislative power
328

ISBN   1 85941 536 9

Printed and bound in Great Britain

FOREWORD

It is inevitable that, at the turn of a century and especially at the turn of a millennium, the role of government and Parliament should become a major focus for discussion. It becomes even more pertinent when, at the end of the 1990s, the world finds itself re-thinking in the most fundamental terms the role and size of the State following the changes of the last 20 years.

In the 1980s and 1990s, many autocratic regimes in Central and Eastern Europe and in developing countries have been replaced by multi-party democracies. With this change, monetarism has become the near-global orthodoxy for macro-economic management. While most governments have reduced the size of their bureaucracies, the parliamentarian in the legislature and the man in the street continue to debate what the 'business' of government should be.

These are questions which the Commonwealth Parliamentary Association (CPA), with experience spanning almost the whole of the passing century behind it, is required by its Constitution to consider. Collaboration with Wilton Park, an independent policy analysis agency funded by the United Kingdom Government's Foreign and Commonwealth Office, permitted us to organise a conference which considered basic questions related to the roles of government and Parliament. For instance, is the job of Parliaments and governments simply to legislate and to balance the budget, or engage in substantial intervention and deficit spending to benefit the economy? Should the State provide such services as education and health free of charge? Which sectors should remain in public control or should almost everything, except a small core of government functions, be privatised? Can governments and Parliaments cope with external factors and events which some would say are increasingly beyond their control?

This book is the official CPA report of the Conference and has been written and compiled by Mrs Priyanee Wijesekera, Deputy Secretary General of the Parliament of Sri Lanka, and Ms Diana Reynolds, Assistant Director of Development and Planning in the CPA Secretariat, who both served as rapporteurs at the Conference. I hope that the issues discussed and views expressed upon them by an eminent and diverse gathering of parliamentarians, diplomats, civil servants and academics will help governments and Parliaments in the Commonwealth and outside it to understand better the challenges with which they are faced.

Arthur R Donahoe, QC

Secretary General

Commonwealth Parliamentary Association

CONTENTS

APPENDICES

CHAPTER 1

INTRODUCTION

In February 1998, the Commonwealth Parliamentary Association, in conjunction with Wilton Park, an Executive Agency of the British Foreign and Commonwealth Office, held the fifth joint CPA/Wilton Park Annual Conference. The 65 participants – who were drawn from a number of countries throughout the Commonwealth, Europe and the United States – included Speakers and presiding officers, members of Parliament, academics, professionals from a range of non-governmental organizations (NGOs) and inter-governmental organizations (IGOs), along with public servants and parliamentary officials.

The theme of the 1998 Wilton Park Seminar was 'The role of Parliament and government in the next millennium'. The conference was held in order to explore developments which might affect democratic institutions in the future and hopefully to identify strategies or solutions to overcome problems which might threaten democracy in the new millennium.

At the end of the 20th century, parliamentary democracy has become the most widely accepted form of government, both in the Commonwealth and worldwide. However, as the close of the 20th century approaches, many consider national Parliaments and governments to have lost the central role they once played in the national life of their countries.

Possible reasons for this include: globalization of the world economy and the concomitant transferring of powers from national Parliaments and governments to supranational organizations; the increasing impact of NGOs and interest groups; the growth of transnational corporations; the revolution in information technology; the privatization of former State enterprises; devolution of power to regional assemblies, and the trans-frontier nature of problems relating to drugs, the environment and crime.

The esteem in which citizens now hold their Parliaments and governments is low. This is partly because of negative media coverage, partly due to corruption (both at election time, and by individual members of government or Parliament), and also in part because of the aforementioned transfer of power from national governments and Parliaments both upwards (to supranational bodies) and downwards (devolution), which leaves the citizenry wondering exactly what is left for their national organs of State to do. This is a major threat to the democratic process, and in part might account for the resurgence in interest in direct democracy.

The greatest challenge for governments and Parliaments of the 21st century will be in developing their roles and mechanisms in such a fashion as to be able to bridge the growing gap between the expectations of the electorate with what governments and Parliaments of the new millennium can realistically deliver. This, then, is the context in which the fifth CPA/Wilton Park Conference was held.

This is the official CPA report based on the proceedings of this seminal Conference. The presenters of the lead papers for each session generously agreed to our utilization of their work in this publication. That said, any errors, omissions or confusions must be claimed as our own.

CHAPTER 2

THE ROLE OF PARLIAMENTS AND GOVERNMENTS IN THE NEXT MILLENNIUM: SETTING THE SCENE[1]

Since the end of the Cold War, a plethora of scholars have advanced a range of theories concerning the future likely state of the world as we enter the new millennium. Some argue that we have just witnessed the final victory of the West (capitalism), and that countries everywhere will now adapt their political systems to those of the West. Others, exemplified by Samuel P Huntingdon in his book, *The Clash of Civilizations and the Remaking of World Order,* argue that the world, for the first time in its history, is now both multi-polar and multi-civilizational. Huntingdon describes a world in which countries increasingly identify their allies and enemies along civilizational lines based on the main cultures and religions, and predicts the possible decline of the ascendancy of 'the west' in the new millennium.

Regardless of which view of the future one espouses, in order to discuss the new millennium and attempt to envisage the role to be played by government and Parliament therein, it is necessary to assume that governments and Parliaments will operate in a largely peaceful world – history has shown that Parliaments play very little role if any in a war situation.

DEMOCRACY AND GOOD GOVERNANCE

It is virtually impossible to define democracy – no definition exists in law and there is no totally accepted consensus over the political meaning of the concept. There are many variants of democracy and different legitimate interpretations deriving from various historical, cultural and regional experiences of the various peoples around the world. But certain features are

---

1   This session was introduced jointly by Mr Arthur Donahoe, QC, the Secretary General of the Commonwealth Parliamentary Association and Mr Anders B Johnsson, then Assistant Secretary General, subsequently Secretary General of the Inter-Parliamentary Union since 1 July 1998, both of whom provided an overview of the current characteristics of government and Parliament in the present century, and attempted to predict the forces, issues and pressures which might influence their development in the future.

common to the concept of democracy as a universal (not exclusively Western) value, argued Mr Donahoe. These include:

(1) the contest of regular free and fair elections (by many parties)[2] conducted by secret ballot on the basis of universal adult suffrage;

(2) there is a separation of powers, an independent judiciary and a free press;

(3) there is respect for the rule of law;

(4) human rights and the rights of minorities are respected;

(5) an independent, efficient and accountable civil service exercises prudent management of public resources.

Underpinning democracy is a private sector free from excessive government intervention.

It was in Harare in 1991 that Commonwealth Heads of Government adopted the now famous Harare Declaration of Commonwealth Principles, which helped establish an international consensus on what constitutes good government. Good government is more than a checklist of different elements, and so cannot be achieved if one of its elements is missing as this will undermine the efficacy of the other elements.

There cannot be legitimacy if those in power do not enjoy legitimacy, are not accountable, allow no channels for dissent, or mechanisms for their own removal at the will of the people. Equally, there cannot be good government if the State, caught in a vicious circle of debt, is unable to deliver the most basic needs of its citizenry, cannot pay its civil servants a living wage, and cannot train them to function efficiently. A good government also does not try to do what the private sector can do better.

Mr Donahoe outlined three universal principles applicable to the concept of good government:

(1) *Competence*: an efficient well trained public service carries out sound economic policies including the operation of a stable currency and creates the legal and regulatory environment to enable the operation of market forces; it must rid itself of corruption, and must ensure that resources are allocated prudently according to sensible priorities. This involves restricting military expenditure to what is necessary and affordable, and giving priority to basics like primary education and health care.

(2) *Accountability*: requires transparency, political pluralism with regular free and fair elections, respect for the rule of law, and free expression, including a free press. A good government respects the people because it is accountable and it ensures that they are able to participate fully in the decisions taken on its behalf.

---

2   This component was disputed in a subsequent session of the Conference.

(3) *Respect for the individual*: this comprises respect for human rights; and an efficient and independent judiciary to give redress to all individuals, rich and poor equally.

Arguing that good government does not require every country to adopt the same model, Mr Donahoe felt it was undesirable that this should happen. Democratic systems in the industrialised world took hundreds of years to build and economic conditions which allowed them to develop are not present everywhere. Every country should choose its own way of practising democracy without being stampeded into models which may not suit its conditions. However, one of the tasks, he continued, is to encourage the necessary mutual respect and tolerance that enables the multi-party system to function and to break down the tendency for oppositions merely to attack the personalities of the existing government and accuse them of oppression, violation of human rights and corruption and of the similar tendency of some governing parties to portray opposition supporters as mere subversives.

Within these basic principles stands the institution of Parliament. It is important to remember that Parliament does not govern – governments govern – but (at least in countries following the Westminster model), Parliament and its members play the vitally important part of providing the people who make up government and of influencing its decisions.

Parliamentary Assemblies are indispensable to any modern vision of democracy, recognising the basic fact that people and their differing views should be fed into and become part of the political process. Every modern democratic State has a Parliament, as do many non-democratic systems.

And yet, many believe that Parliaments are in decline. The diminution of parliamentary sovereignty through membership of regional alliances (such as the European Union), or by unexamined subordinate legislation, or by the rise of quangos, contributes to this perceived erosion. Further, a more educated electorate, a cynical media, the globalization of the economy, the growing influence of NGOs and of single issue groups, the power of political parties, the perceived declining standards in public life and the failure of governments to realise election promises also play a part. These were all advanced as having contributed to a lessening of the public's confidence in their Parliaments.

To be representative, argued the CPA Secretary General, Parliaments must broadly reflect the gender, ethnicity, and religion of the populace. Several Commonwealth Parliaments have taken steps to ensure that women and minority groups are assured representation in their Legislatures. For example, Uganda, Bangladesh and Tanzania, by means of the affirmative action of positive discrimination, guarantee seats for women in their Parliament.

It seems obvious that public faith in Parliament will naturally be reduced if its parliamentarians are perceived to have little in common with the general population.

THE CONGRESSIONAL SYSTEM

Responding to the fact that Parliaments are now widely held in low esteem by the public, some have begun to advocate the introduction of features of the congressional system into the parliamentary system of government. Mr Donahoe explained that these ideas have a superficial appeal as they appear to act as a counter to executive dominance. The central concerns focus on proposals that seek to diminish the ability of the government, first, to dominate the legislative process; secondly, to subject the government party caucus to rigid discipline in support of the executive and legislative initiatives of the Prime Minister and cabinet as the leadership of the governing party; and, thirdly, to exercise the prerogative power of appointment without reference to those members of Parliament or Legislative Assemblies who are not members of the executive.

In the final analysis, Mr Donahoe argued that republican ideas concerning the balancing and sharing of power between separate executive and legislative branches cannot be squared with the basic tenets of responsible government. The American Congress is not a stronger or more democratic version of a Westminster style Parliament. Congress is not a Parliament at all. It is the separate legislative branch in a system where it shares power (legislative and executive) with the presidency (which is the separate executive branch of government). Equally, the President is not the government. The American Congressional model is a fundamentally different system of government to the Westminster model – parliamentary democracy is not a weaker version of the American system, it is completely different.

ACCOUNTABILITY

Many newly elected MPs are deeply disillusioned upon entering the House. Owing to a misunderstanding of the constitutional system in which they operate, many assume they have been elected to govern. This is a misconception. Within the Westminster model, the function of the Parliament is to ensure that the government governs with the consent and confidence of the elected House. This, argued Mr Donahoe, does not mean that backbench MPs (that is, those not in government) are marginal to the practice of responsible government; rather they are crucial in ensuring that the government is held to account.

But, in practice, the accountability function by MPs has left much to be desired. Several reasons for this were identified, including:

- the election of many members who have no parliamentary experience and little or no preparation for their work in Parliament and, accordingly, whose capacity to contribute to good governance within the confines of their roles is well below what is required;

- many of those who do have the ability do not derive satisfaction or reward from engaging in the demanding work required to extract meaningful accounts from ministers;
- insufficient utilization of Question Time;
- absence of ministers at Question Time and in committee sessions;
- excessive control of backbenchers by the party Whip.

Demands for free votes, argued Mr Donahoe, are not testimony to the willingness of backbenchers to act independently, but of their subservience. The right to dissent is always open to every MP, even though it may require defying the party Whip. By such demands, MPs are asking for the right to be independent without having to pay the price. Individually, a dissenting MP has very little impact. Collectively, a swathe of dissenting MPs can bring down governments.

Efforts to impose a kind of public accountability on civil servants in Parliament undermine the constitutional obligations of MPs who are not ministers to demand accountability from ministers. Such designs also bolster a widespread public perception that civil servants are the effective masters of government, thereby absolving ministers of their responsibilities in the public mind.

In order to restore Parliament to a higher place in public esteem, a number of measures were suggested. Amongst these were:

- ministers, assisted by their junior ministers and parliamentary secretaries, should be made to spend more time in appearances before parliamentary committees, providing accounts of their policies and programmes as well as their administration of them. This would require that committees have adequate staff to support MPs in their inquiries, and would provide far more effective scrutiny than can be achieved during Question Time;
- parliamentary secretaries (deputy ministers) should be personally answerable to the Public Accounts Committee for compliance with the law in respect of financial transactions by their departments; and
- the establishment of a parliamentary office of public administration to conduct studies and reviews of general management systems and processes and to report its findings to a parliamentary committee on public administration.

Mr Donahoe urged that the bringing of Parliament's accountability function to centre stage should be a major feature of parliamentary reform in the next millennium.

He also argued that it is essential to open up Parliament and the political process to win back public confidence. Greater public participation in the work of parliamentary committees is a major means of accomplishing this. Members of the public, either as observers of committee proceedings or as experts testifying before them, can become directly involved in the parliamentary process, can learn how the process works, and have direct input into the formulation of policy. Further, because committees operate in a considerably less politically charged atmosphere than the Chamber of the House, a more direct and less partisan detailed scrutiny of the work of the executive is undertaken, which is good both for democracy and the public interest. Effective committee systems are a conduit for mutual education – the public can become better informed about Parliament, and Parliament more receptive to the public's concerns.

Other issues identified by the presenters as possibly impacting on the way Parliaments and governments will change and operate in the 21st century included:

(1) Increased participation of women in public life. While much speculation has taken place as to its consequences, in most jurisdictions, it remains to be seen what effect this will have on the functioning and work of Parliaments.

(2) Another fundamental change which is already occurring is that of the large number of NGOs and special interest groups which have developed in recent years. They were not present when parliamentary institutions were originally established, but are now increasingly interacting with them and seeking to influence their work. The consequences for Parliament are, and will continue to be, manifold, and need to be addressed by Parliament itself.

(3) A growing number of countries have already found it necessary to turn to a bicameral parliamentary system. Whilst a first or popular Chamber ensures the representation of the people, a second Chamber is often necessary to instill a measure of control so that the majority of the day does not automatically prevail over the overall long term interests of all the components of society, be that based on culture, ethnicity, religion or age, or otherwise.

(4) In the same way, the Opposition in Parliament must have the necessary means to participate in the debate, and at least to influence the decisions that are taken. Democracy is not the equivalent of the law of the majority; it resides also in the respect for the rights of the minority. In a large number of countries, particularly those that have only in recent years introduced a multi-party system, this will require setting up some form of status for the Opposition, and granting them the means they require to function properly within the parliamentary institution.

(5) In a world of instant communication, it is hardly conceivable that Parliaments continue to debate the issues of the day far from the eye of the general public. It may therefore be expected that the current trend will continue, and that more and more Parliaments will open up their sittings to direct reporting on radio and TV. Parliaments will also have to deal with the reality of the new information technologies. For example, by establishing e-mail and Internet capabilities for the Parliament and its members, or by permitting audio-visual presentations within the parliamentary Chamber.

(6) Parliaments will need to concern themselves far more than at present with international issues and international co-operation. Many of the problems which today are debated in national Parliaments will increasingly require transnational solutions. Thus, it is in the interests of Parliaments to have a closer involvement in the work carried out in international fora, especially the United Nations.

(7) The transferral of power of national governments and legislatures, upwards to supranational and regional bodies, and downwards to provincial and local decision making bodies.

(8) The possibility of more coalition governments, arising from the increased use of Proportional Representation as an electoral system, or for other reasons. The new millennium may be characterised by increased co-operation between parties. This will require a new method of working – inclusiveness and cooperation, rather than opposition and adversarial tactics.

Participants were agreed that legislators hold in their own hands the potential to improve their systems so as to be able to respond effectively to the challenges of the 21st century.

Participants believed that democracy and democratic principles would become the norm for the new millennium, not least because, as famously observed by the late, great former British Prime Minister, Winston Churchill, in 1947:

> ... democracy is the worst form of government – except all those other forms that have been tried from time to time.

Thus, the stage was set for subsequent sessions of this timely Conference, in which various issues highlighted in this session were explored in greater depth.

MULTI-PARTY DEMOCRACY: THE ONLY POLITICAL MODEL FOR THE NEXT MILLENNIUM?[1]

Although the modern concept of democracy has a distinctive cultural element, its roots lie in the West's established systems of social pluralism and social justice; a shared understanding of the role of civil society and a common belief in the rule of law, along with centuries of experience of working effectively with elected representative bodies. Mr Msekwa in his stimulating paper explored the question of whether multi-party democracy was the only model for democracy in jurisdictions lacking such a long history of shared systems and understanding.

THE ADVANCE OF DEMOCRACY

Quoting Samuel Huntington, an American political scientist, who recently identified three historically separated waves of democratization, Mr Msekwa outlined the rise of democracy in the present age:[2]

> The first long wave of democratization began in the early 19th century, and led to the triumph of democracy in some 30 countries by 1920. Thereafter, renewed authoritarianism and the rise of fascism in the 1920s and 1930s reduced the number of democracies in the world to about a dozen by 1942.

> The second short wave of democratization occurred after the 2nd World War, which again increased the number of democracies to somewhat over 30. But this, too, was followed by the collapse of democracy in many of those countries.

> The third wave of democratization began in Portugal in the mid 1970s, and has seen democratization occur much faster and on a scale far surpassing that of the two previous waves. Two decades ago, less than 30% of the countries in the world were democratic; now more than 60% have governments produced by some form of open, fair and competitive elections.

The 'third wave' of democratization has been characterized by the near universal acceptance of the concept of democracy (as evolved and defined in the countries of the West over hundreds of years), with typically the multi-party variety being seen as being the single most desirable and effective means of governance. This so called 'third wave', argued Mr Msekwa, has

---

1 This chapter is based on the paper presented to the Conference by Hon Pius Msekwa, MP, Speaker of National Assembly of Tanzania

2 Huntington, SP, 'After 20 years: the future of the third wave' (1997) Journal for Democracy, October, p 4 *et seq*.

also seen the apparently successful transplantation and propagation of Western style democracy in regions of the world geographically and culturally far removed from the West. In recent years, for example, many African countries have made successful transitions from one-party to multi-party politics. One question identified by the presenter for the new millennium was 'will multi-party democracy be a universal solution to the sharing of power, or might locally grown alternatives serve particular communities more appropriately and effectively'?

Mr Msekwa maintained that there is strong practical evidence that the current trend is to define democracy in terms of elections, elections being a method of constituting governmental authority and making that authority accountable to the people. A country holding regular free and fair elections, with universal adult suffrage, is deemed therefore to be democratic. Elections are seen as the essence of democracy, which are in turn dependant upon other implied characteristics of democracy (freedom of speech, freedom of assembly, the rule of law, etc). It therefore follows in such definitions that these characteristics can only be guaranteed by a multi-party system.

In Western political culture, the fundamental features of a political party are shared identifiable ideology, good organization, and discipline. This is not always the case in non-Western cultures. Africa can cite numerous examples of would be politicians contesting primaries for one party and, if defeated, contesting for another party on the following day, whilst Asia has had bitter experience of mass defections of members from one parliamentary party to another. In such examples, it seems that the political parties are a mere adjunct to the quest for power rather than the base element in the equation.

Taking elections and the associated characteristics as the essence of democracy, argued Mr Msekwa, is therefore facile. Governments can be elected freely and fairly as described earlier, but if other key features on the political landscape are missing (such as safeguards for individual rights and freedoms like limits on the power of the executive, or an independent judiciary), then such a system cannot be accounted a democracy.

Further, there have sadly been numerous examples where freely and fairly elected governments have gone on to systematically dismantle various democratic safeguards once in office, for example by suppressing their opponents within and outside the House.

Illustrating this point, Mr Msekwa introduced participants to the logic of the Savimbi theory, associated with Angola's Mr Savimbi, which states that:

> If you go into an election, you must win; if you don't win you must have been cheated.

In this context, the defeated party will, by acts of commission or omission, fight against the ruling party which will in turn respond, using State power.

As a result of this, increasingly, the blanket equation of 'democracy' with 'multi-party elections' is being questioned. The definition is being broadened to focus on the need to go beyond the political parties by involving society at large in the democratization process. A strong civil society is required to build and sustain democracy and to act as a check on government. Multi-partyism, argued the presenter, does not guarantee this and therefore does not necessarily lead to democracy.

In a number of countries, election campaigns have provided political candidates with an incentive and platform from which to make appeals of an ethnic or religious nature in order to garner more votes. Such appeals can exacerbate already existing tensions. An account of the political history of Uganda is given later in this volume, which admirably illustrates how ethnic or religious divisions, when translated into party politics, can result in extensive economic, social and political hardship.

The presenter observed that in many developing countries, particularly those which were formerly colonized, the geographic boundaries of the State have little emotional meaning to the citizens. Often, these boundaries were defined by colonial administrators with little regard to the local situation, and therefore have little cultural significance. They may be merely political boundaries. People's relatives are just as likely to live over the border as within it. Therefore, a main concern of such countries is the development, promotion and maintenance of a sense of national unity. In the early days of their independence, many African countries opted for a single party political system as a means of fostering this. Although many have made the transition to multi-partyism, diversity is recognized as potentially a two edged sword – a possible source of strength, or of discord and destruction.

The presenter concluded by questioning the supposition that multi-party democracy is the only political model for the next millennium. There is obviously room for other models to be developed and flourish, as Uganda's non-party movement model shows. It is essential that political systems culturally match their host country. Multi-party democracy is predominantly a Western concept, which operates best in societies where (to paraphrase Balfour on Bagehot) the people are so fundamentally at one that they can safely afford to bicker. Promoting the formation of political parties in order to entrench democracy can result in totally the opposite effect, if such political parties serve to exacerbate existing societal divisions along ethnic or religious lines. This can threaten the unity and solidarity of the nation. Democracy as a political ideology does not require multi-partyism; equally the existence of political parties does not automatically create or sustain democracy.

CHAPTER 4

THE HISTORY OF UGANDA: A CASE STUDY IN THE FAILURE OF MULTI-PARTY POLITICS[1]

By way of illustration to the points made in the earlier paper presented by Mr Speaker Msekwa of Tanzania, the Speaker of the Parliament of Uganda, Hon JF Wapakabulo explained Uganda's Movement System to the conference delegates. This system is essentially a no-party system, developed to allow the holding of elections and to permit the organs of the State to operate effectively without exacerbating tribal or religious hostilities between different groups within the country, as had happened earlier under multi-partyism.

Present day Uganda, which became a British protectorate in 1894, comprises the ancient kingdoms of Buganda, Ankole, Bunyoro, Toro, Busoga, and various other non-kingdom territories bordering Kenya, Sudan, Congo and Rwanda.

THE RELIGIOUS LANDSCAPE

Foreign involvement in the country can be traced back to 1840, explained Mr Wapakabulo, when Arab peoples began to trade with Uganda. British Anglican and French Catholic missionaries entered the kingdom in 1877 and 1879 respectively, when Buganda (the country was renamed Uganda by the colonial administrators) was ruled by King Mutesa I, who insisted that all traders and missionaries operated through the court. Upon his death in 1884, his son Mwanga succeeded to the throne.

The missionary activities of the Anglicans and Catholics, and of the Arabs (who had begun to seek converts to Islam) began to undermine the young King's authority (he had refused to be converted by any of them). The Catholics and Anglicans strove to convert members of the court to their religion, which they did with some success, but rather than influencing the King to also convert, this had the result of estranging the King still further from them, culminating in King Mwanga ordering Christian converts to be burnt alive in 1886. These martyrdoms, rather than ending the spread of Christianity in Uganda, actually fuelled it. In 1888, Christians and Muslims joined forces and deposed King Mwanga. The new King was a Muslim convert.

---

1   Based on a paper presented to the Conference by Hon JF Wapakabulo, Speaker of the Parliament of Uganda.

The remainder of the 1880s and early 1890s were characterized by fighting amongst the three different religious groups. Eventually, King Mwanga was reinstated, with Christian (mainly Catholic) support.

In 1892, the British East African Company – which had been active in Uganda since 1886 – quelled the fighting between the Catholics and Anglicans, and retained the Catholic-sympathising Mwanga as King. His authority was however greatly diminished, as the Anglican Chiefs and missionaries, under the protection of the East Africa Company, effectively controlled the affairs of the kingdom.

The kingdom was divided between the three religious groups, the Anglicans retaining the largest portion. Further disputes between the three powers resulted in the deposition of Mwanga (who had become a Muslim) and the eventual installation of his baby son as King, with three Anglican Chiefs as regents.

RISE OF POLITICAL PARTIES

Once the British had become firmly installed, and Anglicanism ensconced as the dominant religion, the period to 1946 witnessed little in the way of religious or political strife. Uganda's first political party – the Uganda National Congress (UNC) arose in 1952, as an expression of the indigenous Ugandans' objections to European and Asian middlemen commandeering the profits from Uganda's farmers.

The UNC was a Buganda based initiative, led by Anglicans, thereby limiting its appeal for non-Anglicans and people outside the Buganda area. In 1956, the Democratic Party (DP) was formed, predominantly as a protest movement for Uganda's Catholics. A third party, the Uganda People's Union (UPU), developed in 1958 from a core of independent African members of Uganda's Legislative Council, who were opposed to the concessions the people of Buganda district were demanding from the colonial administrators.

By 1959, the UNC had divided into two distinct groupings – one led by Milton Obote (comprising non-Buganda based persons), the other by Ignatius Musazi (Buganda-centric). In 1960, Obote's faction merged with the UPU to form the Uganda People's Congress (UPC), which was essentially an anti-Buganda, Anglican led party. Thus, it can be seen that Uganda's political parties developed along existing religious and geographic lines.

Continuing with his narration, Mr Wapakabulo explained how in 1961 Uganda achieved self-government. In the 1961 elections, boycotted by many, the DP won, its stronghold being in Buganda. Prior to independence in 1962, further general elections were held. The UPC won, with support from the

King of Buganda in an alliance of convenience to oust the DP. Thus, predominantly Anglicans were in government, and predominantly Catholics in opposition.

Developments over the ensuing decade resulted in the deposition of the King and the creation of a republic, the abolition of the traditional kingdoms, major DP defections to UPC and the eventual banning of all political parties but the UPC.

In 1971, General Idi Amin seized power from Obote. He ruled Uganda until his forcible removal in 1979. Rigged elections in 1980 were followed by civil war between Obote's UPC and Yoweri Museveni's Uganda Patriotic Movement (UPM) which developed as the National Resistance Movement (NRM).

Mr Wapakabulo reported how the NRM developed a 10-point plan whilst in the bush. One of the goals of the programme was the correction of past mistakes. The first mistake was seen as being the abrogation by Obote of the 1962 constitutional arrangements which, though imperfect, had nevertheless been agreed upon by the political élite of the time. Secondly, the NRM observed that Uganda's political instability stemmed from the fact that Uganda's social formation was still too primitive to sustain principled multi-party politics. It was observed that European political parties had developed in tandem with social change and that this had not really occurred in Uganda – Uganda is 90% peasantry; the local middle class is very small as is the working class. The attempt to impose multi-party politics in this context, it was argued, had led to the politics of religion and tribe. It was the view of the NRM therefore that Uganda should be governed by a broad based government that encompassed all the political views in the country, until such a time as the requisite social metamorphosis had taken place which would sustain principled party politics.

Therefore, in 1986, the NRM established a broad based government composed of all elements of Uganda's political spectrum. It was hoped that this approach would create an atmosphere of reconciliation very badly needed in a country whose political élite was defined by religion and ethnicity.

In 1987, arrangements were also put in place for direct elections to local councils by the population. Members of the National Resistance Council (NRC) – which acted as the Legislature – were in effect elected by a series of electoral colleagues in ascending levels of local and regional democratic bodies. This process removed power from the Chiefs, who had been the sole source of authority in the villages and towns, and vested it in the hands of the people. Hand in hand with this, a constitution making process was initiated, based on the principle of consultation with and participation by the population. A Constitution Commission under Justice Odoki, a judge of the

Supreme Court, was appointed. The Commission travelled across the entire country seeking views from the population as to what the form of governance should be, including the question of multi-party politics. The overwhelming majority felt political party activity should be suspended, in the interests of peace and development.

Mr Wapakabulo related how four years later the Commission presented its report, recommending that a Constituent Assembly be elected to fully consider the report and to promulgate a new Constitution for the country. This Assembly was duly elected in 1994, and began to consider the Commission's report, whose recommendations included:

- Uganda should never be a one party State;
- the formation of political parties should be guaranteed;
- but political party activity should be suspended for five years, to allow for reconciliation and reconstruction. The question of the resumption of party activity after the suggested five year embargo should be determined by national referendum.

The third recommendation generated controversy in the Constituent Assembly, opponents arguing such a provision was an affront to the fundamental right of the freedom to associate, and also contradicted the other two recommendations. Supporters maintained that it was the sovereign right of the citizens to determine how they should be ruled, and the proposed referendum provided for this. Eventually, all three recommendations were adopted. A referendum will accordingly be held in 2000. Currently, Uganda is practising no-party politics.

PROOF OF THE PUDDING

Under the NRM Government, argued Mr Wapakabulo, there is peace in most parts of the country. The Rule of Law has been re-established and constitutionally guaranteed. The economy has been growing at an average of 6.5% over the last six years. The infrastructure is being rehabilitated and the economy generally is on the up-swing.

In Uganda today, people under the age of 25 constitute the majority. These people do not know first hand the bloodshed and conflict of the past. Their agenda is different – employment opportunities, education for themselves and their children, health services, etc. This, maintained the presenter, is an encouraging state of affairs – where a good section of the population is seemingly primarily concerned with social and economic issues rather than with the politics of religion and tribe.

It will be interesting to see how the people of Uganda will vote in the referendum in the year 2000 – will they opt for a return to multi-party politics, optimistic that the lessons of the past have been well learned and will not be repeated, in the belief that the democracy requires multi-party politics, or will they opt to continue without parties? Only time will tell.

CHAPTER 5

HOW RELEVANT ARE GOVERNMENTS AND NATIONAL PARLIAMENTS IN AN ERA OF GREATER ECONOMIC GLOBALIZATION?

The Canadian High Commissioner in London, Hon Roy MacLaren, PC, a former minister and member of the Parliament of Canada, presented the opening paper on this topic, observing that the direct role of national governments in a broad range of public policy areas has declined in recent decades, and that non-governmental organizations (both national and international) have encroached into this sphere.

He identified some of the many factors creating an environment in which the centrality of Parliament is reduced. These include the following:

(1) Ease of travel and other forms of communication, which has in turn contributed to the rapidly growing globalization of trade in services. This has lead to homogeneity in popular taste, and the creation of a world characterised by consumer dominance rather than producer dominance – hierarchies are being replaced by networks; structures are now horizontal rather than vertical, which legislatures find far more difficult to scrutinize and regulate.

(2) Information technology transcends borders – it permits the gathering, management and dissemination of information worldwide, independent of governments. It facilitates electronic commerce, and the further spread of transnational corporations and the standardization of business practice, values and nomenclature.

(3) The value of private capital flows now far outstrips that of trade in goods and services. New technology is transferring financial influence away from governments to the international market place. The global economy forces national governments into fiscal responsibility – basic economic decisions are made in and by the global economy rather than by national legislatures and Parliaments.

(4) The end of the Cold War has meant the decline of the testing of national policies by Parliaments against the constant threat of latent nuclear hostilities. Defence issues (historically the key area of public policy to which legislatures could lay undisputed claim) no longer automatically occupy centre stage.

(5) Transnational threats (such as environmental degradation, crime, narcotics, corruption, terrorism and poverty) challenge national governments and Parliaments to find new ways of addressing such problems where the demarcation between domestic and foreign policy is increasingly blurred.

(6) The near simultaneous transferral of the powers of decision making and regulation by national governments and Parliaments upwards (to political, social, military and particularly economic supranational organizations) and downwards (to subnational legislatures and local authorities).

(7) The widespread privatization of traditional State enterprises (health, pensions, transport, education) have further limited the perceived relevancy of legislatures, as do government fiscal disciplines (designed to eradicate budgetary deficits, but having the effect of lessening the ability of Parliaments to attempt to manipulate economies through official spending).

(8) The growth in the influence of minority or special interest groups imposes a certain paralysis in legislative action, where politicians and others feel compelled to be 'politically correct', occasionally even at the expense of the collective good and common sense.

Mr MacLaren noted that two totally opposing conclusions have been drawn from the above situation. One school of thought maintains that globalization will lead to the withering away of the nation State, whilst others believe that all these factors underline the need for the development of international rules and supranational organizations which can make and enforce rules for the global economy.

Membership in any rules based international organization requires a transfer of powers, a derogation of sovereignty, thereby reducing the traditional responsibilities of legislatures. This is particularly true in the economic arena, where membership of an economic union must limit the direct powers and responsibilities of national Assemblies.

Mr MacLaren explored the World Trade Organization (WTO) as an interesting example of an attempt to reconcile globalism with a degree of national legislative responsibility.

THE WORLD TRADE ORGANIZATION

The General Agreement on Tariffs and Trade (GATT), the precursor of the WTO, was essentially cast as a contract, to or from which contracting parties could freely enter or depart. There were rules of sorts, but their enforcement was very much within the purview of the contracting parties (that is, national governments/legislatures). Thus, parties found to be transgressing the rules could still block the adoption of Panel reports or the authorization of responsive measures.

In contrast, explained Mr MacLaren, the WTO is a very different animal. It has many more agreed, sophisticated, comprehensive rules, coupled with an effective and automatic procedure for their enforcement. It is a system where contracting parties agreed to forego their ability to block consensus and thus submit themselves more fully to a rules based system.

According to the presenter, the formulation of global rules, fraught with implications for the relevancy of national legislatures, is further complicated by the following considerations:

(a) if the implementation of trade and investment rules has been shifting from national legislatures to international organizations, and if electronic commerce can easily transcend borders, who governs the governors? Should national legislatures have any real role in the formulation, implementation and surveillance of international rules, and if so, how?;

(b) increasingly, the barriers to free trade are recognized as residing in domestic regulation. The traditional role of the GATT (elimination of border restrictions) remains a vocation for the WTO, where national interests may collide with the transcendent nature of global trade and investment liberalization.

The new global economy has many facets. There is international consensus that free market forces are the best prescription for economic growth, and that prosperity must be market-driven. Trade barriers are fruitless and would only accelerate decline. The speed of technological change and increasingly efficient communications are making the world into a global village, thus whole areas of economic activity are becoming decoupled from time and space.

The speed of technological change has contributed to the massive structural change which is occurring to economies throughout the world. New industries are constantly being spawned whilst old ones decline. As markets are deregulated, competition becomes fiercer, and greater prosperity is created.

Mr MacLaren felt that the global economy presents an opportunity to spread more widely the benefits of economic growth. In today's multi-polar world, economic power is becoming widely dispersed, the lines between developed and developing worlds are becoming increasingly blurred. As the British 19th century economist and politician Richard Cobden noted in 1857:

Free trade is God's diplomacy, and there is no other certain way of uniting people in the bonds of peace.

But, asked the presenter, what does all of this mean for the international trading system and the role of national legislatures? Globalization has brought a new agenda into the international trading system. He recalled that only a few years ago trade negotiations tended to stop at the border, being largely concerned with reducing tariffs, or bringing rules based disciplines to bear on other border instruments such as quotas or anti-dumping duties. Today, trade policy is as much concerned with the regulation of domestic industries as with what happens at the border. If domestic barriers are to be reduced or eliminated, then the WTO will have to enter fields long considered the exclusive preserve of national governments (such as trade and investment, trade and environment, trade and competition and trade and labour standards, etc) as the European Union and the North American Free Trade Agreement (NAFTA) have done.

Mr MacLaren explained that as the ambit of international trade rules expands, new demands will be made on the WTO dispute settlement system (one of the successes of the Uruguay Round). The development of this new dispute settlement system is testimony to the willingness of legislatures to transfer upwards to a supranational organization the right to make, implement and monitor international rules in areas where in the recent past national rules largely applied. Countries seemingly now have more faith in the global system and its ability to resolve trade problems.

The High Commissioner noted that international rule making is still in the embryonic stage compared with rule making within national borders (which is decided by national and subnational governments). Also, it is national governments which take the fundamental decisions to make international rules, and therefore the move towards increased multilateral rule making, far from being an erosion of sovereignty, is in fact an exercise of it. Thus, he argued, the process of multilateral institution-building enhances the relevance of domestic governance, and not reduces it.

Elaborating upon this point, Mr MacLaren reported that some 42% of Canada's gross domestic product (GDP) is dependent upon exports – what goes on in markets outside Canada's borders is as important as what goes on within them. The domestic government cannot control economic decisions beyond its borders, but it can influence them through vigorous participation in the multilateral trading system. Mr MacLaren felt that this has long been recognised by Canadians as one of the most relevant activities of their national government.

Concluding his presentation, Mr MacLaren observed that the accelerating pace of change in today's globalized economy presents a challenge of leadership for governments at both domestic and international levels. It is therefore imperative that governments prepare their economies and citizens to compete, whilst safeguarding the expectation that democratic governance will be preserved.

LEVELLING THE PLAYING FIELDS

In the ensuing discussion, some delegates argued that global orders should be truly international, and afford all countries equal opportunity to participate. The extent to which funders of international organizations could influence their agenda was discussed – for example, the USA's withholding its subscription to the UN system impinges upon the effectiveness of the UN. Also, the point was made that large economies (such as China's) had unequal power in international organizations such as the WTO. The question was posed, to which no definitive answer was given, as to whether regionalization and regional bodies might not have a role in redressing some of the imbalances evident in the global arena.

Many delegates felt that transgovernmental networks should be fully international, and not select clubs, which inadvertently dispossessed developing or small countries from their membership. Others were of the view that the interests of small States were often better recognised and protected by rules based organizations rather than by bodies dealing in political power. It was also pointed out that in some instances large NGOs had more clout in the international arena than small states, particularly in terms of monitoring international organizations and that this has some relevance in terms of the so-called democratic deficit that some feel is inherent in supranational bodies.

It was remarked that many multinational companies were worth more than the GDP of many countries. This being the case, the question of how far such transnational organizations were bypassing governments was posed.

One delegate argued that the pursuit of globalization risks the marginalization of State and provincial Parliaments and governments, citing the example of Australia as an instance where this was already occurring. The delegate posited that each time the federal government signed an international treaty or UN Declaration, it is acceding the right to its citizens – and those of other nations – to appeal its decisions in such forums as the International Court of Justice. It is, the delegate argued, also arrogating more power to itself at the expense of the Australian States, by giving itself 'external affairs' power under these treaties, to over rule the decisions of the State Parliaments on issues that are properly their jurisdiction, where such decisions have relevance to the particular international treaty. For example, the Government of Australia signed the Declaration on the Rights of the Child, yet most of the responsibilities for children in Australia fall to the State governments.

CHAPTER 6

DOES DEVOLUTION OF POWER KEEP STATES TOGETHER OR LEAD TO THEIR BREAKING UP?[1]

In political terms, devolution is the handing down of powers from a superior authority to an inferior one; the transfer to a subordinate elected body on a geographical basis of functions exercised by a country's principal legislature or ministers.

Devolution differs from federation in that the powers of the subordinate legislature are conferred by the centre, which retains residual constitutional authority. Under a federal system, the powers of both the centre and the provinces are determined by the constitution. For example, had the Parliament of Northern Ireland been established under a federal model, the British Government would not have been able to prorogue or abolish it as it did in 1972.

Devolution is usually employed to forestall or pre-empt a disintegration, to contain an assertive subculture by conceding considerable autonomy but not full independence. It is intended to keep States together, not to precipitate their break up. Devolution also achieves decentralisation, the dispersal of power and the reduction of the level of government overload. By way of illustration, Dr Lyon presented case studies of Sri Lanka and the UK as a means of exploring whether devolution is a viable solution to political problems.

SRI LANKA: DEVOLUTION AS A SOLUTION TO ETHNIC CONFLICT?

The present population of Sri Lanka comprises some 18 million people. In ethnic terms, the Sinhalese form the majority (73.9%); Sri Lankan Tamils account for 12.7%, and Sri Lankan Moors, Plantation Tamils, and others including Burghers make up the remainder. In religious terms, 69.3% of the population are Buddhist, 15.4% are Hindu, 7.6% are Muslims, 7.6% are Christian, whilst 0.06% practice other religions.

Arguing that analysis of the evolution of ethnic conflict in Sri Lanka suggests that, in addition to issues relating to language rights, and perceived discriminations in employment and university admissions, there was also a

---

1   Based on paper presented to the Conference by Dr Peter Lyon, Academic Secretary and Reader in International Relations at the Institute of Commonwealth Studies, University of London.

growing perception especially from the mid-1980s onwards that the existing system of governance inadequately catered for power sharing between the dominant majority Sinhalese community and the main minority community, the Tamils.

Many political attempts have been made over the years to resolve this point of conflict. For example, the (SWRD) Bandaranaike-Chelvanayakan Pact and the (Dudley) Senanayake-Chelvanayakan Pact, of 1957 and 1965 respectively, attempted to tackle these problems by means of extensive power-sharing, as did the District Development Councils Scheme (implemented in 1981).

These initiatives to bring about a lasting political settlement were further aggravated by the eruption of ethnic-oriented violence in Northern and Eastern Sri Lanka. The 1970s witnessed the rise of several Tamil militant groups, including LTTE (Liberation Tigers of Tamil Eelam), and the Tamil United Liberation Front (TULF).

In 1983, violence escalated to such an extent that country-wide ethnic riots led to a mass exodus of Tamil refugees, predominantly to India, but to other countries as well. What had been a Sri Lankan problem became internationalized.

In 1987, Sri Lanka and India signed an Indo-Lanka Accord. This was designed to encourage the militant groups to enter the democratic mainstream and engage in peaceful competitive politics and speed the surrender of arms by separatist groups. Another outcome of this Accord was the introduction of the Provincial Councils System, in which the northern and eastern provinces were temporarily merged. It also led to the arrival of the Indian Peace Keeping Force (IPKF) to supervise the surrender of arms.

Virtually all Tamil militant groups (except the LTTE) joined the democratic process in the immediate aftermath of the Accord. The LTTE reneged on this understanding and entered into combat with the IPKF. Early in 1990, the IPKF was withdrawn at the request of then Sri Lankan President Premadasa, who had entered into direct talks with the LTTE in an effort to arrive at a political settlement. However, the LTTE went back on their pledges vis à vis the Indo-Sri Lanka Accord and resumed hostilities in June 1990.

A parliamentary select committee to find ways and means of resolving the ethnic problems sat from 1991–93, but no agreement was reached over the interim draft report which recommended a model of devolution similar to that practised in India. Tamil parties participating in the select committee did not endorse the interim report.

Despite this depressing record of past failures, the Peoples Alliance (PA) administration headed by president Chandrika Kumaratunga, which came to power on 19 August 1994 with a clear electoral mandate to seek a lasting settlement, soon set out to produce a solution. This process was accelerated after the presidential elections of 9 November, when President Kumaratunga received an unprecedented 62% of the popular vote, the highest vote ever received in Sri Lanka's electoral history. In Parliament, the government also received the support of almost all Tamil political groups, including numerous former Tamil militant organizations.

Attempting to facilitate the peace process and to alleviate some of the hardships imposed on the Tamil people in the north due to the prolonged conflict, the PA administration relaxed the economic embargo. By April 1995, only eight items considered to be of direct military significance remained banned. This was welcomed by the LTTE leader Prabhakaran. Talks between the government and the LTTE commenced and a Cessation of Hostilities Agreement signed by President Kumaratunga and the LTTE leader Prabhakaran came into effect on 8 January 1995. This Agreement was to be monitored by Peace Communities for each district in the north-east, comprising government and LTTE representatives, and were to be chaired by representatives of the Governments of Canada, Norway and the Netherlands.

After intensive discussion, both within the select committee and among political parties, on 24 October 1997, the government presented to Parliament its proposals for constitutional reform, including elaborate detailed proposals for devolution of power to regions. The implementation of the package will require amendments to the constitution, which in turn requires a two-thirds majority in Parliament, or approval at a nation-wide referendum.

There was continued military confrontation between the government forces and the LTTE thereafter. Politically, President Chandrika Kumaratunga's proposals for devolving power to regional authorities as a way of meeting Tamil demands for autonomy is making slow progress. The main opposition party, UNP, whilst not rejecting the government's proposals outright, has its own notions of how a lasting accord will be brought about. Progress is therefore slow in Parliament and in Sri Lanka's political system at large.

At the time of the 1998 CPA/Wilton Park Conference, Sri Lanka's war with the separatist LTTE was continuing unabated. Devolution proposals had not been implemented, being blocked by violence and a lack of co-operation in Parliament.

In the case of Sri Lanka, should the proposals ever be implemented, it remains to be seen whether devolution will keep the State together, or lead to its breaking up. Militant Tamil separatism, though its enthusiastic supporters are relatively few, still fights for secession, for a separate Tamil State.

[Note by the presenter, February 1999:

In January 1999, Sri Lanka had a violent election for the North Western Provincial Council. Armed mobs stormed polling booths, stuffed ballot boxes and prevented people from voting. Campaigning 'over kill' seemed to be evident when it was announced that the government party had won every polling district and secured 56% of the total vote as against 37% for the UNP. The Election Commissioner reported that over 175 polling stations had been affected by violence and ballot stuffing. Over 50,000 votes were disallowed. Many observers believe that this is an underestimate and that at least 150,000 votes should have been disallowed. Such are the trials of electoral politics in Sri Lanka today.]

UNITED KINGDOM

The question of devolution within the UK was very topical at the time of the Conference, as the new Labour government had committed itself to devolution as a means of enhancing democratic accountability. But, devolution is not a new phenomenon in the UK context.

Six Home Rule Bills (as devolution was once known) were introduced between 1886 and 1920, as a means of providing a solution to the 'Irish problem'. Of these six, the 1920 Bill eventually became law and was implemented – as the Government of Ireland Act. This Act applied only to the six counties of what is now Northern Ireland (counties in which the Unionists could be sure of a majority) – the 26 non-Ulster counties rejected 'Home Rule' and fought for independence, which they eventually secured in 1921.

The devolution settlement in Northern Ireland, was 'a final settlement and supreme sacrifice in the interest of peace, although not asked for by her representatives' as Sir James Craig, the first Northern Irish Prime Minister observed. The devolution experiment in Northern Ireland ended its first phase in 1972 when the British Government unilaterally abolished the government of Northern Ireland.

Devolution re-emerged onto the British political agenda in the 1970s, with the rise of the Scottish National Party (SNP), which before 1970 had never won a seat in a general election. By 1974, SNP was the second largest party in Scotland in terms of votes cast.

A landmark inquiry, whose published two volumes in 1974 are still worth reading for the light it casts on relevant considerations, is that of The Royal Commission on the Constitution (the Kilbrandon Commission 1969–73, Cmnd 5460).

In 1974–75, the new Labour government introduced devolution Bills for Scotland and Wales, which were passed in 1978. Before implementation, however, it was decided that 40% of their respective electorates should endorse the proposals in referendums, which were duly held in 1979. The Welsh population rejected the Wales Act by a 4:1 majority. The Scotland Act secured 33% support. Accordingly, both Acts were repealed, and devolution ceased to be a live feature of the British political landscape as from 1979–97 the Conservative party was in power (a party adamantly opposed to devolution).

In May 1997, 'new' Labour secured office in the general election. It reintroduced the notion of devolution for Wales and Scotland. This time, it was determined to hold consultative (rather than validatory) referendums in Scotland and Wales before drafting devolution legislation. These were duly held in September 1997. The Scots voted 'yes' to the question of a Scottish Parliament by 74.3%, and 'yes' to the question of having tax varying powers by 63.5%. The Welsh declared in favour of a Welsh Assembly by a less strong vote of 50.3%, to a 42.7% no vote. Devolution Bills for both Wales and Scotland were accordingly drafted and passed. The first elections to the new bodies will be held in May 1999, seats being taken shortly thereafter.

The proposals for Scotland provide for a Parliament of 129 members, who will choose a Scottish Executive headed by a First Minister operating in a manner similar to that of the UK Government. The Parliament will be elected using the current German system of proportional representation, with 73 members from single constituencies and the remaining 56 from regional lists.

The Parliament and the executive will be responsible for Scottish domestic matters, broadly, those now under the control of the Secretary of State for Scotland. Powers specifically reserved to Westminster include foreign affairs, defence, fiscal and economic policy, employment legislation and social security. Responsibility for the Constitution of the UK remains with Westminster, so that Edinburgh will not be able to unilaterally alter the devolution settlement. Relations with the European Union will remain the responsibility primarily of the British Government, but ministers of the Scottish Executive will be able to participate in relevant meetings of the Council of Ministers. In some respects, they will be able to speak for the British Government in Europe. The Scottish Parliament will have the power to scrutinise European Union legislative proposals affecting Scotland, and there will be a Scottish representatives office in Brussels to further Scotland's interests in Europe.

The Welsh Assembly will have 60 members, also elected by the German system of proportional representation. Forty will be elected in single member constituencies, and 20 by regional lists. Unlike Scotland, the Welsh Assembly will be led not by a separate executive, but as with local authorities, by an executive committee comprising leaders of its subject committees. The Assembly will be responsible for domestic matters in Wales – broadly, those at present the responsibility of the Secretary of State for Wales. It will not have powers over primary legislation, rules and regulations for Wales, but it will, for example, be able to alter school curricula, or the designation of environmentally sensitive areas within the framework of primary legislation. It will not have tax raising powers.

Neither Scotland nor Wales can achieve full independence (that is, secession) without the nationalists winning an overall majority. Even after that, Westminster would probably insist upon a referendum to test Scottish or Welsh opinion.

Scotland and Wales already enjoy over-representation in the Parliament at Westminster, have Secretaries of State who can argue their case in the Cabinet and receive a favourable financial settlement. The extra political clout which they will gain through devolution will lead to an even more marked constitutional and economic imbalance at the expense, in particular, of under-privileged regions of England, such as the north-east and north-west. It will be interesting to see whether the people of these regions (lacking assemblies of their own) will come to feel themselves second class citizens, and perhaps seek devolution for themselves to protect their interests.

What the present British Labour government is proposing is rolling devolution on the Spanish model. This has three inter-related features. The first is that it is a bottom-up, not a top-down procedure, with devolution being triggered by popular demand. The second is that devolution need not be introduced at the same time for every region of the country, but is to be established only if and when the demand is there. Thirdly, devolution can be asymmetrical. In Spain, the 'historic' communities of Catalonia and the Basque country, corresponding perhaps to Scotland with its own legal system, were given greater powers than other regions without a history of independent Statehood. The Spanish Government has held out the promise of a similar status for Gibraltar in pursuit of its irredentist claim to 'the Rock'.

Devolution then has a dual dynamic. Not only can it serve to contain the threat of separatism in Scotland. It can also, by dispersing power away from Westminster and Whitehall, bring Britain more in line with its partners in the European Union by making it less centralised. Member States of the European Union of a similar size to Britain (France, Germany, Italy and Spain) all have intermediate layers of government, with decentralised power. By contrast, the absence of an intermediate layer in Britain has allowed governments, whether Conservative or Labour, to make Britain the most centralised democracy in Europe, perhaps one of the most centralised in the world.

Britain, then, is engaged in its most profound constitutional transformation since the Great Reform Acts of 1832. Traditionally, the British answer to the question of how to preserve national unity has been to concentrate responsibility and political authority in one supreme authority. But there is an alternative answer – that a society may be held together through what Gladstone once called 'a recognition of the distinctive qualities of the separate parts of great nations'. If that answer is correct, then devolution will strengthen national unity, not weaken it.

Devolution is incompatible with a zero sum conception of politics. Today, it is intrinsically a constitutionalist, consensual, compromising approach to politics. Devolution is not a sovereign remedy for all political situations, but by aiming to produce a new political equilibrium by means of political negotiations and constitutional reform, its processes are tailored to protect the rights of minorities whilst also nourishing participation and power sharing of all the electorate from the grassroots.

The question of whether devolution keeps States together or hastens their break up is very much a moot one. In the present climate, with the exponential growth of regional and global bodies, particularly in the economic arena, size is less likely to be an issue – small jurisdictions can be just as viable as larger ones, provided they lock into the existing global/regional organizations and skillfully practice niche diplomacy and niche economics. But, for Britain today, a central question and test is can a peaceful, constitutionalist form of devolution be made to work for Ulster and therefore for an important part of the UK and of the European Union?

CHAPTER 7

WILL SMALL STATES AND DEPENDENCIES REMAIN VIABLE IN THE NEW MILLENNIUM?[1]

In exploring the issue of whether small States will be viable in the new millennium, the opening speaker explored the concept of size. Germany is small compared with China, and the British Virgin Islands are small compared with Germany. Perceived smallness can also be a product of proximity – a jurisdiction with a population of 500,000 might be deemed large if its immediate neighbours have populations of ten or twelve thousand. However, internationally, 'small' is usually applied to jurisdictions having one million inhabitants or fewer.

Within the Commonwealth Parliamentary Association (CPA) – which has hosted an annual Conference for Parliamentarians from Small Countries since 1981 – 'small' is applied to jurisdictions with a population of 400,000 or less.[2]

The presenter argued that, if criteria other than population size are used to determine what constitutes a 'small State', the picture becomes more complex. Size can be determined by geographical area, economic indicators such as per capita income, or by societal indicators, as per the Human Development Index. Problems of precise definition aside, it was generally agreed that 'small States' were often characterized by many of the following features:

- having a small population (under one million);
- covering a small geographical area;
- having limited resource endowment;
- having open economies;
- having low GDP and GDP per capita;
- having a weak infrastructure;
- inadequate educational and health provision;
- inadequate social provision, with prevailing poverty;
- having a high debt to GDP ratio;
- low direct foreign investment;
- vulnerable social, economic and political systems.

---

1   The opening paper was presented by Hon Erskine Sandiford, MP, former Prime Minister of Barbados.

2   CPA, an association of Parliaments in the Commonwealth, recognizes Parliaments and legislatures in provinces, States, and dependent territories, as well as the Parliaments of the sovereign nations of the Commonwealth. For example, Australia's Norfolk Island with a Parliament of nine members, has a population of 1,500.

The presenter opined that, as the new millennium progresses, doubtless some of these small States will remain the same or deteriorate, whilst others will develop and progress. If present trends continue, wherein rich countries become wealthier, and poor ones descend into an ever increasing spiral of debt, the presenter felt that the prognosis for many small States and dependencies in the coming centuries is not optimistic. The continuation of existing trends, he argued, will lead to an even greater concentration of power and resources in the northern hemisphere, and an increase in poverty in the south.

However, small countries are not necessarily doomed – the quality of their governance can make a huge difference as to how they may fare in the future. In smaller communities, it should be possible to deepen the dialogue between the leaders and the led in a focused and imaginative way. To do so effectively, Mr Sandiford argued, Parliaments and parliamentarians must be well resourced (parliamentary libraries, researchers, use of new technology, use of experts or consultants).

In the past, the viability of small States would have been determined by their ability to defend themselves against land-hungry aggressors. Such scenarios are virtually confined to the past – power is no longer determined by land, or even by wealth. Power in the late 20th century is a product of information and, thanks to advances in communications technology, small jurisdictions are every bit as well placed as are larger countries to exploit this situation.

It was pointed out that, in terms of geographic size, Hong Kong and Singapore are small jurisdictions, yet both are amongst the most successful States in the world, not because of their political environment or commitment to democratic ideals, but because of their having developed an environment conducive to the flourishing of business. They had in effect identified a niche in the market, and had exploited it. The success of these jurisdictions, it was suggested, might be a useful model for other small jurisdictions to emulate in the coming centuries.

It was generally felt that, in political terms at least, dependent territories would not be viable in the 21st century. Despite this, one delegate argued that dependent territories in the Caribbean were far more viable in economic terms than were their independent neighbours.

It was suggested that small countries might have to consider integration with other countries as a means of overcoming some of the disadvantages of size, in federations or confederations, either permanently, or for certain objectives and outcomes. Viability, it was remarked, is a question of balancing the desire to be separate with the political and economic realities of the world. All countries, particularly small ones, need to enter into relationships with others, on a regional or global basis, in order to ensure survival. However, it was noted that in the European context small jurisdictions have had bad experiences of integration with a larger neighbour (USSR).

The perceived advantages of small countries – unity, intimacy and a common culture and outlook – are much envied. Devolution initiatives allow for ethnic or other groupings within a jurisdiction to experience a level of autonomy and intimacy similar to that pertaining in many small jurisdictions, whilst retaining a relationship with a larger power. It was suggested that small jurisdictions which might emerge in the next few years as a result of the modern fascination with devolution initiatives might have an in-built advantage over older small jurisdictions which are completely independent, because of such devolved jurisdictions' special relationship with a 'pivotal State', which might ease their progress and protect their interests in a potentially predatory world.

CHAPTER 8

THE BUSINESS OF GOVERNMENT: HOW LARGE SHOULD IT BE AND WHAT SHOULD IT DO?[1]

Mr Mistry opened his presentation with the following apposite quotations:

> To understand the character of the State, we must assume first that the State does not exist. We may then see why men need a government and discover the kind of government they would naturally establish.
>
> *John Locke, 1671*

> Around the globe, the State is in the spotlight. Far reaching developments in the global economy have us revisiting basic questions about government: what its role should be, what it can and cannot do, and how best to do it.
>
> *The World Bank, 1997*

A BRIEF HISTORICAL OVERVIEW

The presenter explained how in the 18th and 19th centuries the business of government was radically reshaped as democracy emerged in Europe and North America and large parts of Asia, Africa and Latin America were colonized. The colonizing process marked the first major foray into business by imperial governments through highly successful public-private partnerships (East India Company, Royal African Company, etc). The role of government in intermediating between conflicts of interest between capital and labour in the 19th and 20th centuries was further complicated by the increasing importance of overseas trade and the impact of the industrial revolution.

The period 1900–50 was characterized by continuing technology driven socio-economic transformation. The Great Depression, two World Wars and increasing tension between the political ideology of capitalism on the one hand, and communism on the other, added a new dimension to the role of governments everywhere, argued Mr Mistry. From this context emerged European socialism with its emphasis on ensuring human welfare in a market context through government intervention. Variations on this model have emerged as the one adopted by most developing and developed countries.

The European vision of government was characterized by:

- large scale public intervention in the economy;
- the emergence of the welfare state;

---

1   Based on the presentation by Percy Mistry, Chairman of Oxford International.

- State production of public goods and services;
- public ownership, intended to control natural monopolies and suppress the impact of market forces (viewed negatively at the time);
- social re-engineering through the redistribution of income and wealth (by harsh taxation and subsidization of public goods and services).

Mr Mistry stated that the 1980s saw an acknowledgment of the fact that a major imbalance had arisen between the roles of States and markets, which was becoming increasingly difficult to justify or sustain either fiscally or politically. This realization was brought into greater relief by the collapse of communism and the débâcle of third world debt.

FORCES RESHAPING THE FUTURE ROLE
OF NATIONAL GOVERNMENT

Mr Mistry argued that the notion of a nation State exercising sovereign power independently in all matters is now impossible to entertain. He cited the following reasons:

(1) On the one hand, increasingly decisions regarding macro-economic and security issues are falling to the purview of supranational organizations, whilst simultaneously other areas of policy and implementation traditionally reserved to national governments are being devolved to local and provincial bodies.

(2) The traditional major role of national government in the developed world – that of fiscal agent controlling supply and financing demand in education, health care, social services, etc – is becoming untenable. In many areas, it is inappropriate for governments to attempt to do what the market can do better (deliver a broader choice, often more competitively).

The fiscal agency role, if allowed to continue, will increasingly render governments in the developed world incapable of dealing with the real challenges of the nation State, which were seen as being:

- the creation/maintenance of an adequate physical and social infrastructure to compete in a knowledge-intensive world;
- ensuring the ability of the nation to compete globally, by the development of human capital and the creation of incentive frameworks;
- managing the transition of specific traditional functions of national government upwards to supranational bodies and downwards to local and provincial ones;
- coping with the social impact (often deleterious) of technological developments;

- developing adaptive regulatory capacity to ensure fairness, competition and probity in the functioning of all markets, especially financial ones both within and outside their frontiers, and

- ensuring there is a net gain to their societies from the inexorable process of regionalization and globalization;

(3) The concept of the 'developmental State' is a misnomer. In most places, argued Mr Mistry, development has not occurred because the State has misdirected its energies. Confusion about the role of government in the developing world has been compounded by the intervention of international agencies, a relationship which will have to be worked out in the future.

(4) National borders are becoming irrelevant as barriers to transactions in an electronic world. A cyberworld of electronic transactions will raise greater jurisdictional problems, and require a shift in the locus of taxation from income, expenditure and value added to transactions and to the development of formulae and protocols for revenue-sharing across global, regional, national and subnational jurisdictions. As the basis for financing government undergoes a transformation, so will the nature of its business.

THE RIGHTFUL BUSINESS OF GOVERNMENT IN THE NEW MILLENNIUM

The presenter suggested that the next century will in most cases witness a general agreement on the rightful business of government as centring on:

- assuming efficient and cost effective delivery of public services and ensuring a minimum 'safety net';

- completing the first phase of privatization (that is, the total withdrawal from ownership and management of productive assets in industry and infrastructure) and launching a second phase of privatization of the service monopolies (health, education, social services, etc);

- financing assured access to education, health, social services and the like at a minimum acceptable basic level through appropriate policies and funding mechanisms. Governments will need to develop appropriate regulatory capacity to oversee the private sector suppliers of such services;

- organization of an orderly migration of macro-economic and fiscal policy management; external affairs and military security functions to supra-national levels;

- closed national labour markets for unskilled and semi-skilled labour would need to be opened up – enhanced labour mobility; and

- organization of the transferral of micro-management issues concerning social and cultural preferences to subnational levels of government.

In the vision of the new millennium predicted by the presenter, the process whereby the functions of national governance which are gradually separating into two different parts (regional/global and provincial/local levels) will reach its natural conclusion. The mezzanine role of government at the national level will shrink.

Whilst acknowledging that, in theory, the business of government in the politically developing world in the 21st century need be no different to that outlined above, in practice Mr Mistry predicted that the differences between the developed and developing world will continue until the developing countries achieve greater transparency and accountability in their public institutions, and the private interest of public officials is subordinated to their public functions and roles.

Governments in the 21st century in developing countries, predicted Mr Mistry, will cease to own and manage productive assets in industry and infrastructure. Past lack of adequate resources have typically prevented governments in developing countries from playing the fiscal agent role vis à vis social services, etc, and so they will be able to 'leapfrog' into an age of public service provision by private bodies along the same lines as developed countries.

As with developed countries, developing countries too are likely to see some of the core concerns of national government being transferred upwards to regional bodies and downwards to provincial/local bodies.

Just as nation States evolved from the amalgamation of feudal kingdoms and duchies and conquered territories, so the world is poised at the threshold of the next millennium to embark on the next part of its journey of evolution towards eventual global governance, initially by the consolidation of existing regional formations of nation States, and the emergence of new ones in areas where they do not already exist.

Such regional blocs, predicted Mr Mistry, are likely to lead towards a more productive form of constructive multilateralism than that which exists today. Political, social and economic pressures will compel governments to adapt and evolve in order to strengthen their own bargaining positions, even if that means nation States giving way to more powerful regional blocs. For such blocs to emerge, present national governments will need to change their orientations, cope with the opposing faces of macro-economy and micro-ethnicity, and redefine their roles radically regardless of the consequences for national identities or national Parliaments.

In the ensuing discussion, participants commented that as the tide of globalization advances, not all jurisdictions would be successful. Indeed, the number of vulnerable might increase, at least initially. Several delegates were of the view that the single-minded quest for economic development and the implementation of monetarist policies would result in unacceptable social and environmental costs. Equality of opportunity for all people should be guaranteed, even though equality of outcome could not be. Further, they argued that governments should have social objectives and not just be judged in economic terms.

It was noted that traditionally different political parties offered different solutions to economic development. The shape of the future as outlined by Mr Mistry in his stimulating paper suggested, it was observed, a whole new configuration in politics, and a new type of political representation based on consensus rather than opposition. Delegates therefore felt that the development of new parties, based on a platform espousing the benefits of regionalization, could be anticipated. It was suggested that 21st century governments would have to make compacts with the electorate on measurable achievements.

Mr Mistry observed that the picture of government in the new millennium he had drawn was not necessarily one he favoured. It was, however, one he felt would inevitably develop. The reality was that in the past, by attempting to over-ride the market, governments had made such huge mistakes that the market was now reasserting itself. Ultimately, it was a question of balance: in some instances (such as narcotics), governments should override the market; in others (such as telecommunications), it was inappropriate. The market can work well if government regulates it – it is about a nexus – government *and* the market, not either/or.

Government, continued Mr Mistry, is a service function. It should be market driven, not supply driven. Ultimately, the electorate would and should decide what the business of government is, and how large it should be.

Whilst sympathizing with participants, particularly those from Nordic countries (with large governments acting as fiscal transfer agencies of services by means of high taxation), and others anxious for a socialist alternative to the millennial vision he had presented, Mr Mistry maintained his belief that market forces would determine the nature of government in the future, and that those who insisted in swimming against the inevitable tide were likely to be left behind. The only way for governments and national Parliaments to retain their relevance is by swimming with the current of globalization and not against it, he argued.

The session was concluded with the observation that 'the business of government is not business, but government'.

CHAPTER 9

CAN THERE BE FAIRER MEDIA COVERAGE OF PARLIAMENTARIANS IN THE FUTURE?

Two presenters opened this session: Mr Mark Robinson, Director of the Commonwealth Press Union and former Westminster MP, and Sri Lankan member of Parliament Dr the Hon Sarath Amunugama, former Director of the International Programme for the Development of Communication in UNESCO, with responsibility for upgrading communication infrastructure in developing countries. As for all other sessions, other participants included parliamentarians, current or former representatives of the media, academics and civil servants, thus setting the stage for a lively debate.

Interestingly, participants were largely agreed that there was a considerable semantic difference between a 'parliamentarian' and a 'politician', and that the terms are not necessarily synonymous. Parliamentarians, it was felt, are mainly concerned with upholding parliamentary tradition and defending democratic institutions. Politicians, in contrast, are more concerned with the quest for individual and collective power, usually within a party context. The media is typically more interested in politicians that parliamentarians.

The relationship between Parliament and its members and the media is a very sensitive one. Often, MPs complain of receiving unfair coverage in the media, but, it was argued, it must be accepted that they need the media, and the media needs them – as a participant observed, politicians and journalists belong to two mutually unflattering professions!

THE MP'S PERSPECTIVE

Recent elections in the United States and UK, it was maintained, have indicated the primacy of communications strategy, both for the party and the individual politician. As far as the individual elected (or potentially elected) member is concerned, there are several 'publics' he or she must reach:

- constituents: who need to be convinced that, if elected, this individual will represent them well;
- party members: who primarily need to be convinced to adopt candidate x, and that this person will be an asset in the quest to get the party into office;
- the population at large: the general public have to be persuaded of the prospective politician's claim to be a future national leader.

Use of the media is the prime vehicle for contacting all three groups. One participant estimated that a five minute media slot is equivalent to dozens of face to face meetings with the public. However, it is apparently a widely held belief by politicians that the media treats them unfairly on occasion. Specific charges levelled against the media by members of Parliament include:

- non-reporting, or inadequate reporting of their political initiatives vis à vis their different 'publics';
- denial of due prominence;
- poor or non-reporting of their parliamentary activities;
- being unfairly critical, biased or ill informed;
- reporting or quoting out of context;
- placing undue emphasis on sleaze, corruption, etc, which denigrates both the institution of Parliament and its members;
- invasion of privacy;
- vested interests deliberately focusing on the activities of MPs;
- a tendency to trivialize and personalise issues.

In answering such charges, the media would respond that it is duty bound to expose the wrong doings of politicians. Their sales demand good stories, and in the modern world 'good' stories are characterised by scandal, corruption and 'human interest'. It is a sad truth that full reportage of parliamentary debate is no longer considered newsworthy. Increasingly newspapers throughout the world are devoting fewer column inches to parliamentary proceedings, and important initiatives of the government in the field of development are either ignored or ridiculed.

NATURE OF THE MEDIA

The adversarial role of the media is resented by parliamentarians, though in essence this is a critical aspect of democracy – the right to freedom of expression. This watchdog role of the media is safe guarded by law in most jurisdictions (for example, in the First Amendment of the United States Constitution). A free media supplements the role of the Opposition (particularly important in jurisdictions with a weak or non-existent opposition) in that it constantly questions the government and demands accountability.

In many jurisdictions, the Press – still one of the most powerful of media manifestations – is owned by one or two immensely rich and powerful proprietors. A government trying to reduce monopoly/duopoly power would, in such a context, likely be lynched by the Press, and therefore would be well advised not to attempt it. This is an instance in which media coverage might be unfair.

Surveys in the United States and Australia have apparently demonstrated that journalists on the whole have more left wing views than society as a whole. They, therefore, it was argued, promote causes which are not necessarily endorsed by society at large. As a result, politicians who are right-of-centre might automatically receive rough handling from journalists. Further, the agenda of key advertisers can influence the kind of stories a newspapers will cover, and the kind of letters it will print. That said, in many jurisdictions blatantly unfair coverage can be challenged (in court, if necessary) and rectified, by a written withdrawal and apology, and even by financial compensation by way of damages.

The media 'gate keepers' have to sift thousands of bits of information that stream in from provincial, local, national and international sources and select what, in their opinion, is newsworthy. Individual members of Parliament should attempt to develop a media strategy which will increase the chance of their 'story' being picked up and positively reported.

Both parliamentarians and politicians depend on the media to interpret much of what goes on in Parliament and government to the public. Although the existence of Hansard (guaranteed accurate coverage of what an MP actually said in the House) is available in most jurisdictions (in printed form, or increasingly on-line), supplemented in many places by live coverage of parliamentary proceedings on TV or radio, such is for the connoisseur. In order for any message to be widely disseminated to the public, involvement of the media is essential. The ever increasing pace of modern life – the paradox of the 20th century where information gathering and availability of news is virtually at saturation point, offset by the tyranny of the need to be brief – has led, it was argued, to superficiality.

Politicians in many jurisdictions are concerned by an apparent 'dumbing down' of issues by the media. Conversely, criticism is levelled at politicians for their spin-doctoring and practice of statement-by-soundbite (sometimes in the TV studio rather than on the Floor of the House). All this trivialises the business of government and Parliament, feeds the public appetite for superficiality, and escalates the respective sometimes reprehensible behaviour of politicians and journalists alike.

In the recent past, when it was known that a respected parliamentarian was to make a speech in the House, the Chamber would have been packed, both by fellow MPs and by members of the public. Today, in many jurisdictions, virtually the only occasions upon which the Chamber is regularly full is for the brief set piece of Prime Minister's Question Time. The availability of mass communication is moving the actual deliberations of the parliamentary Chamber to a more peripheral position, the media, with its powers of interpretation and dissemination, and ability to get an apposite quotation from a politician is increasingly occupying centre stage. Political battles are no longer won in the Chamber, they are won in the media.

IMPACT OF NEW TECHNOLOGY

The advances in communications technology achieved in the past century have made the media one of the most powerful social forces in the world. Advances in technology have given a greater impetus to the media, and have allowed for greater intrusion. Telephoto lenses, bugging equipment, mobile phones, computer hackers, along with largely uncontrolled publication and dissemination of information on the Internet, means that increasingly matters which would previously have remained secret are now exposed. Every movement, deed, or statement of a politician is potentially being watched and can be reported upon. This can result in increased invasion of privacy. Hence, politicians are anxious to exercise control and influence over the media.

Equally though, these same advances in technology have permitted the enhancement of the media's watchdog role, and also of its mission to inform and educate – for example, satellites permit live broadcasting of debates between government representatives from different countries, or the instant relaying of developments in foreign policy.

The media industry is a very competitive one, in which information is a commodity being traded in the market place. The challenge for parliamentarians and politicians alike is to develop skills which will enable them to utilize the media and make themselves more effective.

The media, it was stated, is driven by profit, power and prestige. In the case of newspaper journalists, the need to sell papers determines the kind of stories they are prepared to cover. Scandal sells papers. Therefore, if politicians engage in behaviour likely to provoke an outcry, they are virtually guaranteed coverage in the Press. Secondly, the media's interest centres on power, particularly on significant MPs (such as party leaders or ministers in key areas like competition policy or privacy) as they may be able to influence them. It is important for parliamentarians and politicians alike to understand what motivates the media, and structure their communications strategy accordingly.

It was suggested that the MP anxious to have his/her initiatives and opinions covered in the media might usefully establish a private news office, and develop his/her own press releases and mailing lists. Indeed, it was noted that a United States Congressman had recently stated that his most important staff member was the Press/PR person, not the case worker.

MPs were advised to nurture good relationships with individual journalists, bearing in mind that a good journalists will always remain a journalist, and never be a true friend. Acceptable tactics recommended for parliamentarians included telephoning newspapers offering comments on particular issues, thereby saving the journalist the trouble of sifting through sheaves of press releases.

The exponential growth of the media industry has meant that narrow-casting (as well as broadcasting) is a viable option. It was felt that MPs should aim to secure coverage in specialist journals, on local radio, in local newspapers and on local cable TV where available, where competition is less fierce, as well as in national and international media vehicles.

The potential of the Internet and e-mail for members anxious for publicity or to set the record straight was noted. It is increasingly easily feasible for each parliamentarian to have his/her own home page on the world wide web, and to distribute updates of his/her activities and concerns to a mailing list of both supporters and critics via e-mail.

The session concluded with a return to the original premise 'Can there be fairer media coverage of parliamentarians in the future?'. Overall, it was agreed that media coverage of parliamentarians in most jurisdictions is already as fair as possible (it was noted that 'media manipulation' is more often the cry of losers than winners), and that to attempt to make it fairer (that is, more favourable to MPs) could impinge upon the essential freedom of the Press. Both the media and members of Parliament are fighting for the same thing – to be opinion formers and societal leaders – hence the tension sometimes evident in their relationship. The media plays an important role in safe guarding democratic values, by its reporting and elucidation of parliamentary and political matters, and by, where necessary, exposing wrong doers.

It was generally agreed that the relationship between politicians and pressmen is a symbiotic one, characterised not least (as one participant wryly observed) by their shared passion for lunching together!

CHAPTER 10

WHAT CAN BE DONE TO COMBAT CORRUPTION AND PUBLIC IMPROPRIETY?[1]

Corruption and public impropriety – major factors contributing to the loss of confidence in public institutions – are apparently endemic, and have assumed a central place in the concerns of many countries and international organizations. Additionally, the globalization of the world and advances in new technology have meant that wrong-doers in one jurisdiction are able to conceal their ill gotten gains beyond their own borders, out of reach of local laws. Unchecked corruption, argued Mr Nzerem, the session presenter, distorts development, particularly in developing countries, and therefore is a major concern for the world, both now and in the coming millennium.

Corruption can be broadly defined as an act or omission, in either the public or private sector, which deviates from acceptable norms governing the performance of official duties, with the intention of creating gain for personal or group advantage. However, it is customary to adopt a narrower definition, namely that corruption is the misuse of public power for private profit.

This last definition assumes that the State has a direct duty to control its own employees, and that it has more scope in its own administration for generating working practices which limit the areas for corruption.

The causes and origins of corruption are often attributed to poverty and culture. For example, in situations where public employees have not been paid for months, they may be tempted, because of economic need, to accept money from others, as a gift or bribe. It would, however, be simplistic to attribute corruption to poverty *per se* – poor people are not synonymous with corrupt people. In some jurisdictions, it is argued that the giving or accepting of gifts to or by public employees is demanded by tradition, despite the existence of laws which criminalize such conduct.

Corruption has a negative effect on sustainable development. Corruption leads to irrational, short sighted decisions motivated by greed rather than need, and to the squandering of resources, for example, where projects are approved on the basis of the short terms gains which will accrue to the decision maker, rather than on the long term gains to the community. This has a detrimental impact upon public confidence in that particular administration, and a concomitant loss of faith in public institutions in general.

---

1   Mr Richard Nzerem, Director of the Legal and Constitutional Affairs Division of the Commonwealth Secretariat made the opening presentation on this subject.

THE NATURE OF CORRUPTION

Mr Nzerem explained that corruption can be extremely difficult to identify. Often, those involved in 'small time' corruption (such as a local postmaster, for example) are more easy to identify and prevent than major actors. Appropriate legislation, coupled with the creation of a culture of accountability, can be very effective in such cases.

However – as the old dictum says, 'power corrupts, and absolute power corrupts absolutely' – political and business leaders can be involved in corruption to an extent which is both far more damaging to society, and far more difficult to identify and therefore to prevent. For example, an elected representative may make a verbal agreement to utilise their official powers to perform a certain action which will redound to the advantage of another individual. There will be no written memorandum of this agreement, and no cash will change hands at the time. The MP will receive his or her pay off many years hence. Such corruption is very difficult to police.

In order to attempt to combat corruption, Mr Nzerem illustrated the necessity of initiatives at the national, regional and international level.

International efforts to combat corruption include, in the Southern and East African Region, an informal Ministerial Group Against Corruption, which was formed in Pretoria in 1994. Its aim is to promote regional harmonization in efforts to combat corruption. Similarly, the Organization of American States has developed a comprehensive hemispheric anti-corruption strategy, whilst the OECD has developed recommendations – relevant to its own members and to the wider international community – to end the practice of tax deductible bribes, and to criminalize the cross-border corruption of public officials.

Transparency International, an agency committed to the elimination of corruption is working extremely hard at both the national and international level. It is defining a code – applicable to both governments and multi-nationals – which will ensure that any company contravening it would be struck off the list of international bidders, and any government permitting corruption would be denied access to international markets. Transparency International operates by forming 'national cells' which strive to pressurize governments to adopt open tendering practices.

Initiatives within the private sector include those of the International Chamber of Commerce, which is endeavouring to strengthen its code of conduct against bribery in international business transactions.

At the United Nations, the General Assembly has sought to revive the ECOSOC initiatives from the 1970s, designed to achieve an international convention against corruption The success of initiatives such as this, argued Mr Nzerem, will depend on the good will of member governments –

international conventions, replete with high ideals and lofty sentiment, need translating by means of local legislation into local law which can be implemented locally.

The first steps, it was suggested, for a national government concerned about corruption would be to take measures within its own borders. These might include:

(1) Promoting an 'open government' approach, by the demystification of government and governmental organs. Initiatives might range from compulsory 'civics' education in schools, supplemented by radio and TV programmes, so that citizens broadly understand how their system of government works, including their own entitlements and duties, along with those of their elected representatives and public servants. Such initiatives could be enhanced by specific programmes at different times, for example, voter education initiatives help ensure the electorate knows not only how to vote, but also appreciate the importance of casting their vote freely, without influence being exerted in the form of bribery or threats.

Additionally, the wide publication of documents such as tax collectors' handbooks would contribute towards creating a more open system, wherein corruption would find it less easy to flourish. Similarly, an expansion of officials' or members of Parliaments' Declaration of Interests to include a statement of not only what they have, but where they got it from would assist in this regard.

(2) Leadership codes, such as the one developed by Transparency International for use in Africa, which spell out the absolute qualities demanded of leaders, including selflessness; integrity; objectivity; accountability; honesty and openness, and leadership are a useful tool.

(3) Reversing the onus of proof with regard to government secrecy. Civil servants and ministers should be obliged to argue why particular documents should not be freely available, rather than, as often happens, citizens having to demonstrate why they should be. Some governments (New Zealand and Belize, for example) have adopted this approach through their Freedom of Information legislation.

(4) Eliminating the areas of and scope for improper behaviour (for example, by the creation and enforcement of rules governing the interface of public servants with members of the public, commercial enterprises, etc).

(5) Privatization, whilst not a panacea, can often be an opportunity for limiting the opportunities for corruption.

(6) Effective monitoring of the assets of public officials.

No single strategy is likely to be effective on its own, but rather an holistic approach is called for, which would require (amongst other measures) a clear commitment on the part of the political leadership to combat corruption, no matter by whom, and the sacking of offenders. The adoption of comprehensive anti-corruption legislation, implemented by a strong and independent agency of manifest integrity (such as an Ombudsman), and prosecuting where necessary, coupled with measures to ensure that adequate remuneration is paid regularly to public officials would help. Also, by ensuring that legal procedures and remedies are such as to provide an effective deterrent (for example, by rendering contracts procured or induced by corruption both void and unenforceable) and forming partnerships between government and the community through its civil society organizations can contribute to the creation of a culture in which corruption cannot flourish.

In the ensuing discussion, the point was forcefully made that the media has an important role to play in exposing corruption. Whistle blowers and persons who leak information about malpractice or corruption should not be penalized. All participants agreed that moral campaigns are more effective than legal remedies, though such campaigns have to be supported by good leadership and sound education for the public.

It was the uncontested view of all participants that in the next millennium neither Parliament nor democracy itself could survive if corruption was allowed to flourish unchecked. The responsibility to root out corruption rests with national governments, operating within the framework of an international programme, as corruption transcends national barriers.

CHAPTER 11

WHITHER THE WELFARE STATE?

Taito Phillip Field, MP (New Zealand) who opened the discussion on this topic gave the participants an exhaustive description of the history of the welfare state in New Zealand, and adeptly rehearsed the arguments for and against the continuation of government subsidies.

He reported that, in New Zealand, as elsewhere, a dominant theme in debates about the welfare state is the issue of 'dependence'. Welfare dependence by certain sectors of society (typically, single parents and the unemployed) is decried as undesirable – for both moral and financial reasons. The current dynamic in welfare reform debate, argued Mr Field, is reverting to that of the deserving and undeserving poor concept, which informed English Poor Law administration for centuries.

The attacks on benefit dependency are based on a number of assumptions, namely:

(1) that, once on benefit, many beneficiaries will remain on benefits for long periods of time, in many if not most instances, permanently;

(2) that those on benefit organise their lives in response to incentives, and negative incentives are required in order to coerce them to behave 'properly' (it was noted that other sections of society – notably the employed – are encouraged to change their behaviour by positive incentives);

(3) that those on benefit have different beliefs and values from the rest of the society – they live in a culture that sets them apart.

All three of these assumptions were demonstrated by Mr Field (on the basis of the research findings of numerous social scientists from around the world) as being totally unhelpful, partially inaccurate or wholly untrue. Social policy made by governments on the basis of the above assumptions, it was argued, is likely to be deeply flawed.

Mr Field persuasively argued that all the evidence indicates that those on benefits want to move from them. What is lacking is not the motivation (as the dependency critics argue) but the opportunity – there is a lack of reliable employment at a reasonable and reliable level of income, supported by the other necessary services such as child care and good quality training opportunities. Without ensuring that such opportunities exist and are maintained, the poverty of social security would merely be swapped for the poverty and uncertainty of inadequate wages.

Mr Field reported that it is generally agreed that there are three distinct types of modern welfare state operating in the world today.

RIGHTS BASED (SOCIAL CITIZENSHIP) MODEL

This model is based on the idea that a healthy democracy needs to ensure that all of its citizens can participate fully in community affairs and in the political process, and that social services should be available to maintain a person's membership of society, as of right, regardless of accidents or misfortunes such as sickness or unemployment. Scandinavian countries, such as Sweden and Denmark, offer the most successful and complete examples of the rights based, social citizenship model.

INSURANCE BASED

The second model, the insurance based welfare state, is one in which the size of an individual's previous contributions to a fund determines their level of support, rather than the person's actual need. This model originated in 19th century Germany, and still predominates there and in many other European countries including Austria, France, Italy, and The Netherlands. This type of welfare state favours those in paid employment, and discriminates against those who are not (such as women caring for children at home), so most modern states find it necessary to provide means tested assistance for those unable to contribute to welfare or superannuation funds. In these 'conservative welfare states', economic and social policies are viewed as complimentary, within a framework of strong social controls.

RESIDUAL OR MINIMALIST MODEL

The minimalist welfare system is one in which the state provides only a 'safety net' for the very poor and needy, and expects most citizens to provide for their own welfare needs in the marketplace or from charities. This is the classical liberal ideology of self-reliance and individual responsibility which is today best exemplified by the USA. The residualist or 'safety net' doctrine has been revived in recent years by theorists of the New Right, who criticize the rights based welfare state for sapping individual initiative and distorting the free play of market forces in the economy. Such critics claim that the rights based welfare state is too expensive and ultimately unsupportable in the post-Keynesian world economy.

Traditionally, the New Zealand welfare state largely corresponded to the first of these models, but not as completely as Sweden or Denmark. New Zealand governments, continued Mr Field, have been wary of insurance based schemes, so the second model of the welfare state never took root, but means testing for some benefits made the New Zealand system something of a hybrid incorporating elements of the rights based and residualist models. In contrast, recent changes in policy have seen a programme of welfare reforms with a new emphasis on individual obligations and responsibilities.

In concluding his presentation, Mr Field asserted his belief that it was the right and proper role for government to invest in people (health, education, housing, etc), and to provide a safety net of social benefits for those unable to provide for themselves, through unemployment, ill health, age or other reasons.

The account of the development and expansion of the welfare state in New Zealand, and the recent curtailment in expenditure in many traditional areas, was a phenomenon recognised by many participants as the welfare system in their own jurisdictions had expanded and contracted along similar lines.

Several participants argued that the time was right for urgent modification of the welfare state. It was argued that governments should not themselves supply the various social services, rather they should confine themselves to the formulation and oversight of social policy, and the provision of a basic 'safety net', leaving the actual delivery of social services to be provided by the private sector. Market forces employed in social service delivery, it was believed, would provide the end user with more choice, and would probably be more cost effective.

In contrast to the experience of many participants from Western democracies, an Australian observed that the welfare state in Australia was still expanding. The amount per citizen on social welfare spent in 1961–62 had tripled by 1995–96. The percentage of Australians on pension or benefits had more than doubled between 1970 and 1996, and, if people employed by the government are added to these figures, delegates were told that a picture emerged of more than 40% of the Australian population aged 15 and over being dependent on the government.[1] This, the delegate argued, is not only economically unaffordable, but also is inefficient (on the basis that when people get something for nothing demand inevitably outstrips supply, which may result in governments having to make sudden, massive adjustments), and is unaccountable (government as both service provider and regulator is likely to be less motivated to yank the proverbial skeleton from its closet). Arguing that the welfare state, with the goal of equality of outcome has failed,

---

1   Figures from Warby, M, 'Equality, justice and sustainability: the failing logic of the welfare state', in Goldsmith, M (ed), *Social Justice: Fraud or Fair Go?*, 1998, Canberra: Menzies Research Centre.

the delegate urged for the development of a system of social welfare focused on the more achievable goal of equality of opportunity.

Thus, proponents of the two main opposing schools of thought on the future of the welfare state argued their cases. Supporters of the political right's 'minimalist' approach defended a system which targeted the 'deserving poor' to provide a minimum standard of living. Defenders of the social democratic 'maximalist' approach maintained that social welfare is the inalienable right of all citizens, and should not be given at the state's discretion or whim.

Participants from developing countries noted that economic considerations in their jurisdictions had prevented government from providing very much in the way of a welfare state to their citizens. In such countries, many of the social services provided by the state in more affluent jurisdictions were voluntarily provided by the extended family and community. Thus, family members helped nurse the sick and tend the aged. Unlike in many places in the West, where economic realities were leading to the down scaling and privatization of welfare services (sometimes, a deeply difficult political decision to sell to the public), developing countries in the millennium would be able to avoid the trap of even attempting to have government supplying such services, and instead move immediately on to developing the regulatory framework so that private enterprise could deliver the same.

CHAPTER 12

WOMEN IN PARLIAMENT AND GOVERNMENT: INTO THE NEW MILLENNIUM

This Conference session took the form of a presentation by a panel, followed by general open discussion. The panellists were: Hon Pius Msekwa, MP (Speaker of the National Assembly, Tanzania); Tuulikki Petäjäniemi (Director of the Centre for Finnish Business and Policy Studies, Finland); Lorna Smith (Permanent Secretary, Office of the Chief Minister, British Virgin Islands); and Grethe Rostboell, MP (Denmark).

For democratic institutions – including Parliaments and governments – to be truly legitimate all sectors of society must be represented, including women. In most of the world's parliamentary jurisdictions, the right for women to vote in and stand for election has been well established for many decades. Yet women are still significantly numerically under represented in most national decision making forums. That so few women have assumed seats in the Parliaments and legislatures of the world, and even fewer have gone on to assume ministerial or parliamentary office, is one of the greatest concerns of the late 20th century.

The year 1975 was declared International Woman's Year, and the decade 1976–85 was designated the International Decade for Women. Four United Nations Conferences focusing on women were held between 1975 and 1994. Within the Commonwealth, successive Declarations of Heads of Government since at least 1991 have committed this association of over one quarter of the world's population to the principle of equality for women. The 1997 Commonwealth Heads of Government Edinburgh Communiqué (Report of the Committee of the Whole) noted:

> ... Ministers Responsible for Women's Affairs had reviewed progress in the implementation of the 1995 Commonwealth Plan of Action on Gender and Development (CPAGD) at their meeting in Trinidad and Tobago in November 1996, and had adopted a set of recommendations which they encouraged member governments to implement according to their circumstances and in keeping with the CPAGD. They noted also that the establishment of gender management systems and the strengthening of national women's machineries were central to the effective implementation of the Plan of Action and that ministers had urged governments to strengthen measures to integrate gender into macroeconomic policies, particularly budgetary processes, and to ensure that women are recognised as a specific target group, especially with regard to poverty alleviation and other programmes.

The Committee recommended Heads of Government endorse the proposal made by ministers that member countries should be encouraged to achieve, in ways most appropriate to their national circumstances, a target of no less than 30% of women in decision making in the public and private sectors by the year 2005, and that governments should increase women's participation in all peace initiatives.

Thirty per cent is a minimum target; not an absolute goal. It is generally accepted that 30% is the 'critical mass' for women's representation, and that that level of representation having once been reached it is unlikely that such gains would not be sustained.

Vast amounts of research has been undertaken in an attempt to identify the factors which prohibit women from entering the political arenas of their countries, or which make them reluctant to even contemplate such a move. Affirmative action, quotas, reserved seats and other mechanisms have been identified and employed to attempt to redress this imbalance, yet still in most jurisdictions of the world in the late twentieth century women constitute only a tiny minority of the membership of most decision making bodies, at the local, national and international levels.

Delegates to the CPA/Wilton Park Conference were hopeful that the new millennium would be characterised by a significant increase in the number of women winning elections, and occupying positions of governmental or parliamentary significance. In order for this to come to pass, existing barriers must be eradicated.

BARRIERS

In many countries in the world, the State is unable to provide free education. In such instances, if parents have to make a choice over which child they will send to school, cultural and traditional factors determine that the male child is more likely to be given the opportunity. Even in wealthier countries, where education is provided free to all children, cultural and traditional attitudes mixed with academic rationality tend to permeate the school curriculum, with the result that boys traditionally emerge from the process as more assertive and confidant than the girls. A career in public life requires amongst other things self-confidence.

Typically, women assume prime responsibility for bringing up the next generation, and for looking after the sick and aged. This state of affairs imposes a triple burden on women – their time is totally taken up with family concerns; they are confined to the ambit of the household and denied the opportunity to 'network' in the way working men do, and they are economically dependent upon another adult – they lack financial resources of their own. Thus, often, women (especially young ones) do not have the time, contacts or cash to make even the consideration of a political career an option.

Because membership of most of the world's Parliaments is male, Parliaments naturally have a male ambience, which many women find off putting. Parliamentary sitting times are often not conducive to family life and most Parliaments do not have crèches. Multi-partyism often manifests itself in the Chamber in violent verbal assaults and aggressive posturing between the opposing sides, which a lot of women find alienating. Also, because there are so few women in decision making forums, there are correspondingly few positive role models for women.

Some delegates were of the view that the demands of globalization and devolution would contribute towards the development of a different kind of politics: less adversarial and more inclusive, with a greater emphasis on the identification of common ground and shared solutions between the different parties in Parliament. It was felt that such a political climate would be more attractive to women.

QUOTAS

Several countries have constitutional or legal provisions to ensure women's presence in their national decision making bodies. Fifteen of the 225 parliamentary seats in Tanzania are reserved for women, as are 30 of Bangladesh's 330 seats.

In other jurisdictions, the initiative to take positive action to ensure women's participation in Parliament has been taken by the political parties, which have developed their own regulations to ensure that a certain number of women are adopted as electoral candidates, sometimes with a proviso that a certain number of 'winnable seats' be specially reserved for women candidates. Initiatives such as these, coupled with training programmes by political parties and NGOs for prospective candidates, help assist women to overcome the barriers and so become parliamentarians.

Those in favour of quotas, reserved seats and other affirmative action measures intended to get more women into Parliament argue that such measures are necessary to change the political landscape which traditionally favours males. Quotas ensure that a minimum number of women get to Parliament and that those women in Parliament are not totally alone in that male-dominated arena. Advocates of quotas argue that if the system mitigates against women securing nomination and election in their own right, then new systems should be devised to 'level the playing field'. Proponents argue that a female perspective is required in Parliament, that men cannot adequately represent women and that women's equal representation in Parliament is a right which is not being upheld. Hence, some form of affirmative action is therefore justified. However, many hoped that quotas will prove to be a temporary 'pump-priming' mechanism which hopefully should rapidly become obsolete.

Opponents to affirmative action measures such as quotas argue that they are undemocratic and unfair. They fear that women fast-streamed into Parliament by such schemes are likely to be less qualified and effective than parliamentarians who got into the House on their own merit, and that such weak role models will be damaging to the perception of women MPs. They find the implication that only females can represent females adequately deeply insulting.

One delegate from a developed country reported how she had been adamantly opposed to quota systems as a means of ensuring representation for women, until her attendance at a CPA Conference, at which she heard the testimony of women members from developing countries. These women had recounted how the economic, educational and cultural barriers in their countries were such that, without affirmative action, no woman would ever be elected to Parliament. This had persuaded her that quotas were a necessary evil in some circumstances.

A delegate from Estonia remarked that, under Communism, women had made up 50% of the work force and had comprised half of the Supreme Soviet. Since the collapse of Communism, women were apparently not anxious to secure work outside the home nor to become actively engaged in politics. This was interpreted by some as evidence that men and women are fundamentally different, and that women naturally gravitate towards the private sphere of the home. Others interpreted such a state of affairs as having arisen because men had seized the positions of power, to the detriment of women.

The point was made that targets, quotas and other mechanisms to increase the number of women in decision making forums was not merely a question of integrating women into the existing world of men, but rested on the belief that a world in which women were playing a full and equal role in all areas of life – including politics – would be a better one. The issue is far more complex than merely achieving gender parity in Parliament and government, though obviously this is key, as parliamentarians make the laws that define and change society.

Parenthood, it was argued, should not be seen as a female occupation – men make good parents too. Nursing and teaching should not be viewed as women's work, nor building or engineering as exclusively male preserves. By assigning by law, practice, tradition, culture or convention different mutually exclusive roles to the two genders, the whole of society is being needlessly confined and limited. By undervaluing the work performed by certain sectors of society – particularly women (one delegate said that the UNDP had estimated that if the unpaid work performed by women was ascribed a monetary value, it would add $3 trillion to international accounts!) – a skewed vision of society was being presented and perpetuated, to the detriment of us all.

A delegate from Denmark was able to report that, in her country, Parliament is 37% female, and 25% of government ministers were women. No formal barriers exist to prevent women from succeeding in politics, education or business, but lots of informal ones (tradition, family, gender interaction) still played a role.

Finnish women have a saying 'Nordic women are on top of the world'. Finnish women achieved the right to vote in and stand for election in 1906, and, one year later, 19 of the 200 seats in Parliament were held by women (a figure standing at 67 out of 200 at the time of the conference). Fifty two per cent of Finland's wage earners are women, and, typically, they occupy full time posts – they are not in a marginalized sector of the job market. Sixty per cent of all university places are occupied by women, and, as a nation, the Finns are now concerned lest men become marginalized. Initially, when there were relatively few women in the Finnish Parliament, they tended to focus on matters of specific concern to women. As increasing numbers have entered the political arena, their interests have broadened – at the time of the Conference, women held the posts of Speaker, Minister of Foreign Affairs and Minister of Defence.

Democracy is not democracy if women are excluded from playing a full role in local, national or international decision making forums. Over one hundred years after the first country gave women the right to vote in and stand for elections, across the world, women are still seriously under represented in Parliament and government. The setting of international targets, the implementation of national quota systems and party initiatives, coupled with the vast amount of study and research being undertaken to identify new strategies and approaches would, it was hoped, see the new millennium emerging with representative numbers of women occupying positions in government and Parliament, and making a concomitant contribution to good governance.

DIRECT DEMOCRACY: A GROWING THREAT TO NATIONAL COHESION AND DEMOCRACY?

Dr the Hon Marlene Goldsmith, MLC (New South Wales, Australia), opened the discussion, observing that the concept of direct democracy had been enjoying a resurgence in recent years, its attraction apparently centring on the fact that it goes straight to the people, and not through an elite.

There are basically three varieties of direct democracy: the initiative; the referendum; and the recall. Discussion was restricted to the referendum.

Those who support participationist as opposed to Westminster style democracy argue that it is by the direct participation of citizens through referendums that this is best achieved. New technology means that it is now possible to recreate the situation pertaining in ancient Greece, the cradle of democracy, where every enfranchised person had a direct input into the business of government. Interestingly, representatives from small jurisdictions argued that their small face to face societies meant that the lines of communication between the rulers and ruled were very open, and that consequently direct democracy per se had no role to play in their jurisdictions.

Participants identified a number of possible reasons for the resurgence of interest in direct democracy, including:

- public disillusionment and dissatisfaction with parliamentarians and the institution of Parliament itself;

- a feeling by some that minority or special interest groups are not well represented in Westminster style democracies;

- a feeling by others that minority and special interests are over represented in Parliament (politicians are dependent on winning elections, elections are often won by attracting marginal/floating voters, politicians therefore seek the support of these marginal voters by promising to vote for legislation such groups favour, thereby weighting the legislative process in favour of interest groups, particularly those which are well organized and well funded); and

- the fact of the existence of new technology with its potential applications for direct democracy.

Dr Goldsmith presented a hypothetical scenario (for which the technology already exists) in which every citizen, carrying a micro-computer/phone on their person, would be swiftly and easily contacted in order to ascertain their views and opinions on various referenda questions. Safeguards would prevent any individual from voting twice, and also could ensure that each citizen accessed relevant web pages (prepared by government, lobbyists, or other interested parties) before voting. Utilising new technology would mean that the opinion of all citizens could be sought on all manner of issues, and the results swiftly collated and declared.

The ensuing discussion centred upon why the electorate might feel they were better equipped to directly govern themselves, rather than be governed by the duly elected representatives in Parliament. Accordingly, an exploration of the 'added value' parliamentarians and Parliaments bring to the democratic process was initiated.

ADDED VALUE

Parliamentarians, it was argued, are professional decision makers, able to devote far more time to the consideration of issues of State than might the average citizen being canvassed by electronic referenda. Parliamentarians are able to shape and lead opinions, thereby encouraging a gradual transformation in society.

It was asserted that decisions reached in Parliament arise from a consensus mechanism which would be entirely lacking in keypad referendums. Decisions reached in Parliament allow for the initial proposal or proposition to be substantially modified during the course of the debate – referendums do not permit this. Referendums, it was argued, reduce issues down to the starkest of yes/no, lowest common denominator factors, and do not allow for synthesis of the original proposal by different shades of opinion in the way that Parliament does.

Many delegates, believing that the role of government is to make society more competitive, argued that government by referendum would work against this, both for the reasons outlined above and because the public is notoriously conservative. It was also argued that one of Parliament's key roles – the examination of the operation of government and other institutions and the calling to account thereof – could not be replicated or replaced by any existing form of direct democracy. Parliamentarians, and the institution they inhabit, is therefore necessary.

Two schools of thought emerged regarding the issue of whether direct democracy, particularly referendums, is a threat to national cohesion. Some questioned whether referendums could be any more of a threat to national unity than Parliaments themselves already are, arguing that most Parliaments are structured to reward conflict – the opposition scores if it criticises the government; parliamentary processes stress differences, not commonalities. Conflict is a threat to national unity.

Others felt that national cohesion is under greater threat by the fact that national Parliaments have handed economic affairs upwards to supranational bodies, and local matters/ethnicity issues downwards to local Assemblies, than by referendums.

Conversely, others argued that the instruments of direct democracy – the initiative, the referendum and the recall – if used wisely and sparingly in relation to selected, fundamental issues, could make a useful contribution towards enhancing national cohesion, by ensuring the citizens themselves directly gave their support to key changes and developments.

At the conclusion of this very lively and interesting discussion, delegates were broadly agreed that direct democracy would not replace existing forms of democracy in the new millennium, but would become a more important adjunct to it.

CHAPTER 14

PROMOTING EFFICIENCY IN PARLIAMENTS

This chapter is based on two separate Conference panel sessions. The first addressed the question of 'Promoting efficient and independent administrations in Parliament', and was introduced by Mr Willem Hendrik de Beaufort, the Clerk of the Second Chamber of the States General, The Netherlands. The second addressed the question of the applications of information technology within Parliaments, and was opened by Helen Irwin, Principal Clerk to the Select Committees, House of Commons, UK.

EFFICIENCY IN PARLIAMENTS

Mr de Beaufort argued that efficiency is not the prime criterion to be applied to parliamentary administrations. Parliaments should be judged on their output or results – that is, by the quality of the society in which they are located. If, as was argued, one of a Parliament's prime vocations is to resolve conflict, a country with few strikes or riots is probably a country in which the parliamentary institutions are working well. In such circumstances, it was maintained, the public will not question whether the money being spent on Parliament is really necessary, or question too closely the institution's efficiency.

That said, many legislatures provide numerous examples of atrocious inefficiencies. For example, the European Parliament currently meets in three separate places: in Strasbourg, in a building shared with the Council of Europe; in Luxembourg; and in Brussels. Each venue can accommodate 700 in plenary, and all three have sufficient office space to meet requirements. Yet a new palace is currently being built in Strasbourg, so that the European Parliament will not have to share its accommodation. This inefficiency (being multi-located) has been institutionalised – France signed the Maastricht Treaty on the basis that there would be 10 sessions held in Strasbourg – and has arisen as a result of political compromise.

Another similar apparent example of inefficiency cited by the presenter can be seen in the case of the German Parliament. Currently, the Parliament is based in Bonn. Although this building has been extended numerous times in the past 10 years, it was recently decided that the Parliament should move to Berlin, and be accommodated in a new building. Cost wise, this is probably not a good decision, yet apparently the majority in German political life feel it is important to have Parliament housed nearer the former East Germany, for symbolic reasons.

At first glance, continued Mr de Beaufort, many of the most fundamental practices and procedures of Parliament appear to promote repetition and duplication and, as a result, could be construed as inefficient. For example, where there are many parties in a Parliament, each party will study each piece of legislation individually, and usually each will discover exactly the same things. Similar duplication is apparent in parliamentary questions, where separate oral and written questions may seek to elicit the same information. Such 'inefficiencies', it was argued, are necessary, as part of the parliamentary checking and balancing mechanism.

Parliaments' inquiries can be expensive, in terms of calling witnesses and paying for researchers. Further, it can sometimes be the case that, after an extensive and expensive inquiry, no substantial result is forthcoming. Yet, this too should not be considered inefficient, as the provision to hold inquiries is actually more important than achieving a measurable outcome.

Traditionally, legislative procedure is considered the core business of Parliament. In many democracies, the notion of efficiency when applied to legislative procedure is translated into the need to control time, to have a timetable.

In some countries, such as the UK (where ministers are MPs), the government controls the timetable. In Holland, the rules of procedure control the timetable. For example, Dutch Standing Orders state that a committee to which a Bill is referred must make a decision regarding the last date by which it will receive submissions, and must report this date within 14 days of the Bill's having been referred to it. The Bureau of the House sets the time for the committee's report to be published. Before the Standing Orders were changed, committees tended to work on and on and without ever giving back a legislative proposal to the House. This was inefficient.

It was noted that, in some countries, such as those which have recently achieved independence, a large amount of new legislation needs to be drafted and passed quickly. In such circumstances, the limitations on MPs and the committees must be greater, and there might be a tendency to delegate law making to the government. Participants opined that it is important to question at what and at whose cost this happens.

Participants were told that, in Tanzania, it is accepted that the majority of parliamentary business is government business (on the basis that the election gave the government a mandate and therefore it takes priority). It is the duty of the Speaker or Business Committee to cooperate and enable the government to carry out its mandate, and therefore the faster laws are passed the better. On average, Tanzania adopts 30 pieces of legislation every year, some of which is brand new, and some of which is by way of amendment. The main business has to be government business, and it has to take precedence: the parliamentary administration should be geared to that, it was argued.

Delegates agreed that speed is not the only efficiency criterion for legislative procedure. Other values are important. It is a question of balance in making the right choice.

It was observed that deliberate abuse of parliamentary procedures can lead to inefficiency. For example, governments can use the 'Order of the Day' to stifle controversial debate by the opposition, or filibustering can be employed to stifle progress.

THE OFFICIALS AND STAFF IN PARLIAMENT

The independence of parliamentary officials is key in ensuring the efficient and effective running of Parliament. Delegates were agreed that from the cooks and ushers upwards, staff should be appointed without regard to their political views, the political party of the government or Speaker, or to nepotism. In Holland, this notion was formalised in 1989 when the Clerk was given the power to make 95% of the appointments. Similarly, the Ugandan 'Administration of Parliament' Act establishes a parliamentary commission which appoints staff, but delegates this power to the Clerk for officials at lower grades.

It was generally agreed that, in the interest of efficiency, Parliaments should not be over staffed. Staff numbers should not be determined by peak periods. Additional staff should be temporarily employed for particularly busy times or for special projects.

Independent staff provide an element of continuity in Parliament, which can be essential. For example, it was remarked, in the Dutch context, that at the time of the Conference 120 of the 150 MPs in Parliament had not been in Parliament four years previously. It was predicted that the next elections would result in there being fewer than 10 MPs in the House with more than five years' experience – hence, the importance of independent staff in providing continuity.

THE MEMBERS

It can be argued that the efficiency of Parliaments (as a tool for holding the executive to account, and as a means of passing effective and relevant legislation) is mainly determined by its membership. Many Parliaments and political parties run induction courses for new MPs, in order to help them operate effectively as parliamentarians and as politicians.

The Commonwealth Parliamentary Association has developed considerable expertise in holding post-election seminars for newly elected MPs, many of whom may lack any previous parliamentary experience. Typically, by invitation, an international five member CPA team runs a parliamentary workshop over a three or four day period, designed to familiarize members with their new rights, duties and responsibilities, and the basics of parliamentary practice and procedure. The story of the development of the Commonwealth as a vibrant organization committed to the promotion of democratic ideals is an integral part of the programme.

Several delegates observed that increasingly Parliaments are handling international relations. Only 10 years ago, international contacts and overseas travel for parliamentarians might have been viewed as tourism. Today, it is largely recognised that Parliaments and their members require an international perspective.

The importance of supranational decision making was repeatedly stressed during this Conference, and it was agreed that Parliaments need to ensure that MPs know and understand supranational structures. Ignorance about such bodies can lead to a Parliament's either becoming, or being perceived as inefficient or irrelevant. Similarly, delegates were of the opinion that Parliaments should ensure that their members are equipped to fully exploit the potential of international parliamentary institutions (such as the CPA, the IPU, AIPLF, the Council of Europe, etc).

INFORMATION TECHNOLOGY

The late 20th century revolution in information technology (IT), which has transformed the way in which business is conducted throughout the world, is often being under utilised, or adopted very slowly in many of the world's Parliaments. That Parliaments as national communication centres could benefit immensely in terms of efficiency and (in many cases) cost effectiveness by the utilisation of new technology was generally agreed by all Conference participants. In most cases, although the initial hardware investment is expensive, IT operation costs are low, and savings on traditional forms of information dissemination (such as printing and posting) can be considerable.

Increasingly, many new members of Parliament are already familiar with the capabilities of computers in general, and the Internet and e-mail in particular, from their previous occupations before entering Parliament. In many cases, the IT capacity of the Parliament is far behind that of the commercial world from which the member came. However, this state of affairs seems to be gradually changing.

More and more Parliaments now have made available (or are in the process of doing so) official House publications on the world wide web (www). This enhances efficiency – Hansard on line or on CD-Rom is searched far more easily by electronic means than by the traditional manual approach of flicking through an index. Lists of members of Parliament, along with biographical data, can be updated daily on the web, thereby being perpetually up to date and accurate (unlike with printed lists, which relatively speaking take a long time to produce, and soon become permanently outdated). At its best, IT can offer instant accessibility and accuracy.

Conversely, as many participants noted, no society in the world is yet in a position to produce information exclusively in electronic format alone, without also making the same data available in traditional printed forms, so as not to disenfranchise those without IT access. Further, IT start up costs, in terms of hardware purchase and software upgrades, and Internet access are prohibitive for some Parliaments. Finally, information available on the web is never absolutely safe from being tampered with by hackers – a big issue for Parliaments in terms of security and accuracy issues.

Despite such concerns, IT is already beginning to be harnessed by many Parliaments around the world, which are recognising and embracing its potential as a tool for enhancing public understanding of Parliament and the democratic process.

Information technology is a two-way street. Parliaments can disseminate information by means of it, and likewise can receive information from and through it. For example, it was explained that in the House of Commons at Westminster each member is provided with a computer, which is linked to the main parliamentary computer network. This allows them to access various parliamentary databases, and parliamentary publications through the intranet, and to access the Internet. E-mail facilities – both internal (within the Palace of Westminster) and external – are also provided. Gradually, members are exploiting the capacity of e-mail as a means of keeping in touch with their constituents during the week. Similarly, it was reported that MPs in The Netherlands use the Internet to hold private referendums to ascertain public sentiment on a variety of issues.

A cursory search of the Internet will reveal that increasing numbers of MPs the world over are maintaining their own web pages, onto which they place information about themselves and their activities. This useful form of self-promotion is enhanced by the gradual development of individual e-mail mailing lists, which enables MPs to despatch circular missives to limitless numbers of individuals in his or her electronic constituency.

It was pointed out that new technology does not merely allow for the automation of existing processes. It allows for the development of entirely new ways of doing things. For example, parliamentary debates of the future may well be enlivened by photographic images, or tables of relevant data summoned to a screen in the Chamber by an MP in order to illustrate the point with a few key strokes on his lap top! The Australian State of Victoria – which must be one of the most committed IT utilisers in the world in order to enhance citizen interaction with the organs of government and Parliament – already accepts colour photographs in its electronic Hansard.

In conclusion, although efficiency in Parliament is not of prime importance, it was generally agreed that the increased application of new technology in several areas of parliamentary work would enhance both the institution's and its members' ability to access and disseminate information. This, it was believed, would enhance the ability of individual MPs and parliamentary staff to perform their duties, and would contribute to an increased awareness of the business of Parliament by the public.

CHAPTER 15

FINANCING POLITICAL PARTIES:
CAN AN EQUITABLE SYSTEM BE DEVISED?

Equity is the fundamental principle which should inform all democratic institutions. Both electoral systems and electoral divisions should reflect an equitable representation of the political forces behind the electorate, rather than the economic forces. A neutral electoral administration is key to this. These were the introductory points made in the opening presentation of Hon Jean Garon, MNA, of the National Assembly of Quebec, Canada.

As regards financing political parties, Mr Garon argued that the principle of equity operates in ensuring that the richest parties are not given a louder voice merely because of their financial status. Procedures should be developed which allow parties and candidates to gather political funding in an open, fair and accountable way.

In Quebec, the Election Act governs party financing, under the guidance of the Chief Electoral Officer, an official appointed by the National Assembly. This means that the office holder is exclusively answerable to the National Assembly, via a parliamentary committee.

THE HISTORY OF PARTY FINANCING IN QUEBEC

The 1875 Election Act, reported Mr Garon, marks the earliest legislative provisions governing party finance in the province. Under the terms of this Act, political candidates were required to appoint an official agent to handle their expenses (this requirement lapsed in 1932), and, from 1895, were required to publish a statement of election expenses in the Official Gazette (lapsed in 1926).

In the period following the expiration of these requirements, the years 1932–63 were characterised by there being no requirement to declare election expenses, and there being no provision to oversee how candidates/parties were operating. This naturally provided an opportunity for corruption to flourish – for example, money being given to political parties in exchange for 'favours' once the party was in government, such as the awarding of government contracts and the like.

In 1963, a new Election Act was promulgated, which restored the candidates' obligation to name an official agent for his or her election expenses. Further, a ceiling was placed on party/candidate expenses, and a system instituted wherein the government reimbursed a proportion of the expenses incurred by those elected, and of those candidates who had secured 20% of the popular vote in the election, even if not returned to Parliament.

Quebec adopted its first statute on political financing in 1975, by which government granted an annual allowance to all parties in the National Assembly, thereby guaranteeing a measure of public financing for political parties. In 1977, an Act regarding party finance – with particular reference to funding by individuals and businesses and the requirement for transparency – became law.

This 'Quebec Model' in which public and private finance for political parties is rationalized, with safeguards to ensure transparency and equity, is characterized by the following:

THE 'QUEBEC MODEL' OF PARTY FINANCE

- The government pays authorized parties an allowance (determined by a formula involving the number of votes cast for that party at the last election) to cover expenses incurred in administrative costs, in publicity, and in the co-ordination of the political activities of their membership. This allowance is paid monthly, upon presentation of receipts and accounts to the Chief Electoral Officer.
- Further, political parties are reimbursed 50% of the cost of their annual financial audit (to a ceiling of $5,500).
- Election expenses are reimbursed by the Chief Electoral Officer to a ceiling of 50% of the actual costs incurred by political candidates securing 20% of the vote in their constituency, or who were successfully elected at this or the previous general election; and to the candidate who is the candidate of either of the two most successful parties in that constituency at the last election. The fact that reimbursement is based on present and previous election results, explained Mr Garon, creates a modicum of stability regarding the financing of splinter groups, and extends public financing to parties other than the two main ones.
- Political parties are reimbursed 50% of their election expenses. Each party's expenses are limited to 50 cents per elector in all electoral divisions in which that party is fielding candidates. Certain candidates (those for whom the final amount to be reimbursed can be calculated at the outset) can claim expenses in advance.
- In Quebec, electors are given a tax incentive for contributions made to political parties, to a maximum credit of $250.

Public financing aims to supplement and stabilize party revenues, making it unnecessary for candidates/parties to be indebted to individuals or businesses for their election.

In Quebec, only individual electors are allowed to make financial contributions to political parties, to a maximum of $3,000 per annum. Businesses, corporations, unions or special interest groups are prohibited from making financial or contributions in kind/services to political parties.

Political parties are allowed to generate income through the holding of activities, providing the entrance fee is no more than $60 per day.

This diversified financing system characteristic of the 'Quebec Model' allows political parties to maintain their independence from big business and wealthy individuals.

PARTY POLITICAL MEDIA COVERAGE

In Quebec, the media is not obliged to give air time or space to political parties free of charge. However, if the media does decide to grant a political party a platform, it must extend the same privilege equitably to all parties represented in the National Assembly, and to those unsuccessful parties at the last election which nevertheless gained 3% of the popular vote. During election time, the Canadian Radio, Television and Telecommunications Commission – an independent organization charged with the remit of regulating broadcasting – issues directives to the electronic media to ensure equity of coverage for all parties.

The Quebec Election Act prohibits any partisan publicity in the seven days immediately following the calling of an election, in order to limit any strategic advantage the incumbent party may have.

It was pointed out that the finest of legislative provisions can become a dead letter if mechanisms do not exist to monitor and enforce compliance with the law. In Quebec, both provincial political parties and their local party authorities must produce audited financial reports, detailing the name and address of each elector contributing more than $200. These reports are available to both the public and media.

Further, the Chief Electoral Officer has the power to survey and control party financing and electoral expenses. He or she has the power to investigate inquiries, and to prosecute transgressors in court.

In concluding, Mr Garon asserted that the 'Quebec model' demonstrates that it is possible to establish an efficient and equitable system of party financing based on contributions by the people.

In the ensuing discussion, participants noted that in developing countries a system which relied so heavily upon funding by individual electors would not work well, as individuals probably would be unable to afford to contribute. It was further observed that the 'Quebec model' favoured a multi-party system in which there were only two viable contenders for government.

Political parties are likely to remain an integral part of the democratic fabric in the new millennium. Initiatives, such as that of the province of Quebec – which has striven to ensure that political parties are independent of big business, maintain close links with their electors and have open and accountable processes of financing – are likely to become blueprints for other jurisdictions in the future. Properly and equitably financed political parties are one means of ensuring a level political playing field and of building public confidence and involvement in the democratic institutions of a jurisdiction, which, participants were agreed, is necessary for the effective functioning of Parliaments and governments in the next millennium.

CHAPTER 16

WHAT IS THE ROLE OF PARLIAMENT IN PROTECTING HUMAN RIGHTS?

The opening presentation was made by Richard Bourne, Chairman of the Commonwealth Human Rights Initiative Trustee Committee, London, who argued that the key characteristics of a democracy included:

- regular elections by secret ballot on the basis of universal adult suffrage;
- separation of powers and a free press;
- respect for the rule of law;
- existence of an independent, accountable and efficient civil service managing public affairs; and
- respect for human rights and the rights of minorities.

Parliament occupies a key place within any democratic system and as such has a huge role to play in the protection of its citizens' human rights. However, it should be noted that Parliament is not the only body with a role to play in this area; Non-Governmental Organizations, other civil society bodies, members of the judiciary, lawyers and barristers and the media share this responsibility.

Parliament impacts upon human rights by means of a variety of its roles:

(1) *Parliament as legislator*

Parliament's prime function is the making of laws and, in so doing, it often has to balance the needs and rights of one group against those of another – for example, legislation regarding the right to privacy has to balance the rights of the individual with the requirement that the Press in a democracy should be free.

Secondly, Parliaments should ensure the compliance of local laws with tenets of international conventions, including those relating to human rights. For example, Art 5 of the Vienna Declaration, which represents the agreed global position between sovereign States and human rights, states:

> All human rights are universal, indivisible and interdependent and interrelated. The international community must treat human rights globally in a fair and equal manner, on the same footing, and with the same emphasis. While the significance of national and regional particularities and various historical, cultural and religious backgrounds must be borne in mind, it is the duty of states, regardless of their political, economic and cultural systems, to promote and protect all human rights and fundamental freedoms.

(2) *Parliament as budget approver*

Ultimately, Parliament holds the governmental purse strings. This function gives Parliament huge power and by wielding it wisely it can ensure that various human rights (such as the right to education, the right to medical assistance, etc) can be met, by awarding the requisite budget.

(3) *Parliament as a body demanding accountability from government*

A key function of a Parliament is to hold government to account. Question Time and debates, for example, can be used to highlight instances in which human rights have been denied or violated, both at home and overseas.

Some Parliaments in the Commonwealth, in order to ensure that women, the disabled and ethnic minorities are able to play an active role in decision making at the highest level, have adopted a system of reserved or nominated seats for such groups. Such measures, it was argued, help redefine the norm, whereby women and representatives of minority communities are seen as having the right to play a full role in national decision making, and the Parliament itself is seen as being truly representative of the whole nation.

In addition to Parliament and parliamentary committees, independent oversight institutions such as Human Rights Commissions, Ombudsmen and Electoral Commissions play an important, complimentary role in the protection of human rights. In order for such bodies to be able to work effectively, it is essential that they are adequately funded and equipped, and able to operate independently. It was deemed important that Parliaments should set aside adequate time to fully consider the reports of such independent oversight bodies.

Although Parliaments, by making laws which protect and promote human rights (such as legislation regarding domestic violence, or freedom of information legislation), it was repeatedly noted that stringent local laws and international conventions are useless without ongoing monitoring for compliance, proper enforcement and swift trials for transgressors.

Human rights are vulnerable if people do not know what their rights are. Public education campaigns, and the inclusion of a 'civics' component in school curricula can help eradicate ignorance thereby contributing to the creation, promotion and maintenance of a culture of human rights. The right to information is fundamental to good governance ensuring as it does accountability, transparency, and effective participation. The free flow of information ensures parliamentarians are more attuned and responsive to their constituencies, and can effectively represent their interests and can be seen to do so.

In general, parliamentarians themselves could make a greater impact on human rights by:

- promoting a culture of human rights in their own countries;
- supporting the efforts of NGOs and civil society;
- favouring systems of governance that further equality, pluralism, the accommodation of diversity, gender sensitivity and popular participation;
- adopting models of development which are compatible with the practical realisation of individual human rights and human dignity.

It was remarked that human rights are vulnerable if people do not know what their rights are. Public education campaigns, and the inclusion of a 'civics' component in school curricula can help eradicate ignorance thereby contributing to the creation, promotion and maintenance of a culture of human rights.

CHAPTER 17

CONCLUSION

The week-long conference raised many issues of relevance, and though widely different views were expressed, on many matters there appeared to be agreement on the basic principles.

Most participants expressed a strong belief in the market economy, particularly after the collapse of the socialist economies. The necessity of having welfare benefits to cushion the adverse effects of social crises cannot be denied. Yet it has also to be recognized that the State cannot cope with extensive welfare measures and that there is a limit how far the State should be involved in the delivery of social services.

The increasing power and importance of the media is a cause for much concern among parliamentarians. Yet everyone agreed that censorship would be counter-productive. As regards corruption, all were agreed that the only hope of stamping out corrupt practices was by national and international initiatives aimed at catching wrong doers, closing loop holes and creating a culture of accountability in which corruption would be unable to survive. This was felt to be one of the most difficult challenges the new century would face.

Fears regarding the 'democratic deficit' some saw as an inherent feature of supranational bodies were expressed, but overall participants accepted that future developments were likely to result in an increased number of supra and subnational bodies, and that the simultaneous development of such bodies would result in better government and greater accountability to the people. Women were fully expected to play a much larger role in governance in the new millennium.

For national Parliaments to continue to retain their validity in the coming millennium, it is necessary that legislators continue to search for improved methods of functioning and administration, particularly as regards the applications of the new information technology. Parliaments it was felt, where financially feasible, should be amongst the first to utilise new technological developments, not the last.

There was no lack of ideas expressed on how to improve parliamentary democracy. It was agreed that any such improvements can only be effected with a great deal of will and commitment from those who participate in the political life of their countries now. The ultimate challenge for the new millennium will be to entrench and improve on existing democratic institutions in the light of new threats and demands.

APPENDIX I

PARTICIPANTS AT THE CONFERENCE

PARTICIPANTS AT THE CONFERENCE

THE ROLE OF GOVERNMENT AND PARLIAMENT IN THE NEXT MILLENNIUM

Monday 23–Friday 27 February 1998

PARTICIPANTS

AJOJE, Abiodun

NIGERIA

Minister Counsellor, High Commission for the Federal Republic of Nigeria, London

AMUNUGAMA, Sarath
(Speaker)

SRI LANKA

Opposition Member, Parliament of Sri Lanka, Sri Jayewardenepura Kotte

BARAL, Lok Raj

NEPAL

Professor of Political Science, Department of Political Science, Tribhuvan University, Kathmandu

BARBAROSIE, Arcadie

MOLDOVA

Deputy Rector, Academy of Public Administration, Chisinau

BATES, T St John N
(Visiting Speaker)

ISLE OF MAN

Clerk of Tynwald, Legislative Building, Douglas

BLIZNACHKI, Georgi

BULGARIA

Associate Professor in Constitutional Law, University of Sofia, Sofia

BOSTWICK, Henry

BAHAMAS
President of the Senate, Nassau

BOURNE, Richard
(Visiting Speaker)

UNITED KINGDOM
Chair, Commonwealth Human Rights Initiative Trustee Committee, London

BRADY, Christopher

UNITED KINGDOM
Senior Lecturer in International Relations, Joint Service Command and Staff College, Bracknell

de BEAUFORT, Willem
(Speaker)

NETHERLANDS
Clerk of the Second Chamber of the States General, The Hague

DHAR, Meenakshi

COMMONWEALTH PARLIAMENTARY ASSOCIATION
Assistant Director, Conference and Management Services, CPA Secretariat, London

DONAHOE, Arthur

COMMONWEALTH PARLIAMENTARY ASSOCIATION
(Co-Chairman) Secretary General, Commonwealth Parliamentary Association, London

EICKMEYER-HEHN, Annette

GERMANY
Deputy Head of Division 316, Federal Ministry of Education, Science, Research and Technology, Bonn

EL HAGE, Juliette

UNDP
Programme Management Officer, Human Development and Statistics, Regional Bureau for Europe and the CIS, United Development Programme, Bratislava

FIELD, Taito Phillip
(Speaker)

NEW ZEALAND
Member, Select Committee for Social Services, New Zealand Parliament, Wellington

GARON, Jean
(Speaker)

CANADA
Member, Parti Quebecois, National Assembly, Quebec City

GEORGES, Elton

BRITISH VIRGIN ISLANDS
Deputy Governor, Tortola

GOLDSMITH, Marlene
(Speaker)

AUSTRALIA
Legislative Council, Sydney

GOMEZ, Raja

COMMONWEALTH PARLIAMENTARY ASSOCIATION
Director of Administration, CPA, London

HARVEY, Paul

UNITED KINGDOM
Deputy Head, Africa Department (Equatorial), Foreign and Commonwealth Office, London

HATFULL, Martin
(Session Participant)

UNITED KINGDOM
Head, Commonwealth Co-ordination Department, Foreign and Commonwealth Office, London

HAVLICEK, Ivan

CZECH REPUBLIC
Deputy Chairman of the Senate, Prague

HOPKINSON, Nicholas
(Co-Chairman)

UNITED KINGDOM
Senior Associate Director, Wilton Park, Steyning

HUSSAIN, Baboo Ghulam

PAKISTAN
National Assembly, Parliament of Pakistan, Islamabad

IRWIN, Helen (Visiting Speaker)	UNITED KINGDOM Principal Clerk, Select Committees, House of Commons, London
JASKIERNIA, Jerzy	POLAND Deputy Chairman, European Integration Committee, Chairman Polish-British Parliamentary Group, Warsaw
JENNINGS, Colin (Co-Chairman)	UNITED KINGDOM Chief Executive and Director, Wilton Park, Steyning
JOHNSSON, Anders (Visiting Speaker)	INTER-PARLIAMENTARY UNION Deputy Secretary General, Inter-Parliamentary Union, Geneva
JONES, Jenny	UNITED KINGDOM Chair, Executive Committee, Green Party of England and Wales, London
KERSTGES, Andrea	GERMANY Deputy Chief Editor, German Parliament, Bonn
KLEMENCIC, Andrej (Session Participant)	SLOVENIA National Assembly of the Republic of Slovenia, Ljubljana
LAVERDIÈRE, Hélène	CANADA Deputy Director, Policy Planning Staff, Department of Foreign Affairs, Ottawa
LILLOE, Vibeke	NORWAY Consul, Norwegian Consulate General, Edinburgh
LYON, Peter (Visiting Speaker)	UNITED KINGDOM Academic Secretary, Institute of Commonwealth Studies, London

MacLAREN, Roy
(Visiting Speaker)

CANADA
High Commissioner, Canadian High Commission, London; former Minister for International Trade, Ottawa

MATAURE, Michael

ZIMBABWE
Chairman, Parliamentary Reform Committee, Harare

MAUERHAN, Franck
(Session Participant)

FRANCE
Journalist, 'Le Bien Public', Dijon

MISTRY, Percy
(Speaker)

INDIA
Chairman, Oxford International, Milton-Under-Wychwood, Oxfordshire

MSEKWA, Pius
(Speaker)

TANZANIA
Speaker, Parliament of Tanzania, Dar Es Salaam

NZEREM, Richard
(Visiting Speaker)

COMMONWEALTH SECRETARIAT
Director, Legal and Constitutional Affairs, Commonwealth Secretariat, London

OKEKE, Uche

NIGERIA
Acting High Commissioner, High Commission for the Federal Republic of Nigeria, London

ONATE, Santiago

MEXICO
Ambassador, Embassy of Mexico, London

PETÄJÄNIEMI, Tuulikki

FINLAND
Director, The Centre for Finnish Business and Policy Studies (EVA), Helsinki

PLUMMER, Lynne
(Interpreter)

UNITED KINGDOM
Interpreter, Foreign and Commonwealth Office, London

PODOBNIK, Janez
(Session Participant)

SLOVENIA
President, National Assembly of the Republic of Slovenia, Ljubljana

POMPON, André

MAURITIUS
Clerk of the National Assembly, Port Louis

QUARTERMAN, Richard

UNITED KINGDOM
Tutor, Individual Staff Studies Course, Joint Services Command and Staff College, Bracknell

REYNOLDS, Diana
(Rapporteur)

COMMONWEALTH PARLIAMENTARY ASSOCIATION
Assistant Director, Project Development, CPA Secretariat, London

ROBERTS, Matthew Vernon

ST LUCIA
Speaker, House of Assembly, Castries

ROBINSON, Mark
(Speaker)

UNITED KINGDOM
Executive Director, Commonwealth Press Union, London

ROSTBOELL, Grethe

DENMARK
Conservative Member of Parliament, Folketinget, Copenhagen

RUDLOFF-SCHÄFFER, Cornelia GERMANY
Head of Section, Federal Ministry of Justice, Bonn

SANDIFORD, Erskine
(Speaker)

BARBADOS
Member of Parliament; Former Prime Minister of Barbados, Bridgetown

SEVER, Mjusa
(Session Participant)

SLOVENIA
Adviser to the President, National Assembly of the Republic of Slovenia, Ljubljana

SINIJÄRV, Riivo   ESTONIA
                                    Ambassador, Estonian Coalition Party,
                                    Tallinn

SMITH, Lorna   BRITISH VIRGIN ISLANDS
                                    Permanent Secretary, Office Of Chief
                                    Minister, Tortola

SMITH, Ethlyn   BRITISH VIRGIN ISLANDS
                                    Legislator, Realtor and Accountant, Office of
                                    the Legislative Council, Tortola

SZAJER, Jozsef   HUNGARY
                                    Vice President, Young Democrat Party,
                                    Budapest

TONELLI, Simon   COUNCIL OF EUROPE
                                    Administrator,   Employment   Unit,
                                    Directorate of Social and Economic Affairs,
                                    Council of Europe, Strasbourg

UIMONEN, Risto   FINLAND
                                    Journalist, 'Heisingin Sanomat', Helsinki

van der VEEN, Roelof   NETHERLANDS
                                    Policy Planning Staff, Ministry of Foreign
                                    Affairs, The Hague

WAPAKABULO, James   UGANDA
(Speaker)   Speaker, Parliament of Uganda, Kampala

WIJESEKERA, Priyanee   SRI LANKA
(Rapporteur)   Deputy Secretary General, Parliament of Sri
                                    Lanka, Sri Jayewardenepura Kotte

WING, Donald   AUSTRALIA
                                    Member of Parliament; Vice Chairman.
                                    Commonwealth Parliamentary Association
                                    Executive Committee, Launceston, Tasmania

APPENDIX II

DECLARATION OF COMMONWEALTH PRINCIPLES

DECLARATION OF COMMONWEALTH PRINCIPLES

The Commonwealth of Nations is a voluntary association of independent sovereign States, each responsible for its own policies, consulting and co-operating in the common interests of their peoples and in the promotion of international understanding and world peace.

Members of the Commonwealth come from territories in the six continents and five oceans, including peoples of different races, languages and religions, and display every stage of economic development from poor developing nations to wealthy industrialised nations. They encompass a rich variety of cultures, traditions and institutions.

Membership of the Commonwealth is compatible with the freedom of member governments to be non-aligned or to belong to any other grouping, association or alliance.

Within this diversity, all members of the Commonwealth hold certain principles in common. It is by pursuing these principles that the Commonwealth can continue to influence international society for the benefit of mankind.

We believe that international peace and order are essential to the security and prosperity of mankind; we therefore support the United Nations and seek to strengthen its influence for peace in the world, and its efforts to remove the causes of tension between nations.

We believe in the liberty of the individual, in equal rights for all citizens regardless of race, colour, creed or political belief, and in their inalienable right to participate by means of free and democratic political processes in framing the society in which they live. We therefore strive to promote in each of our countries those representative institutions and guarantees for personal freedom under the law that are our common heritage.

We recognise racial prejudice as a dangerous sickness threatening the healthy development of the human race and racial discrimination as an unmitigated evil of society. Each of us will vigorously combat this evil within our own nation. No country will afford to regimes which practise racial discrimination assistance which in its own judgment directly contributes to the pursuit or consolidation of this evil policy.

We oppose all forms of colonial domination and racial oppression and are committed to the principles of human dignity and equality. We will therefore use all our efforts to foster human equality and dignity everywhere, and to further the principles of self-determination and non-racialism.

We believe that the wide disparities in wealth now existing between different sections of mankind are too great to be tolerated; they also create world tensions; our aim is their progressive removal. We therefore seek to use our efforts to overcome poverty, ignorance and disease, in raising standards of life and achieving a more equitable international society. To this end, our aim is to achieve the freest possible flow of international trade on terms fair and equitable to all, taking into account the special requirements of the developing countries, and to encourage the flow of adequate resources, including governmental and private resources, to the developing countries, bearing in mind the importance of doing this in a true spirit of partnership and of establishing for this purpose in the developing countries conditions which are conducive to sustained investment and growth.

We believe that international co-operation is essential to remove the causes of war, promote tolerance, combat injustice, and secure development among the peoples of the world; we are convinced that the Commonwealth is one of the most fruitful associations for these purposes.

In pursuing these principles, the members of the Commonwealth believe that they can provide a constructive example of the multi-national approach which is vital to peace and progress in the modern world. The association is based on consultation, discussion and co-operation. In rejecting coercion as an instrument of policy, they recognise that the security of each member State from external aggression is a matter of concern to all members. It provides many channels for continuing exchanges of knowledge and views on professional, cultural, economic, legal and political issues among the member States.

These relationships we intend to foster and extend, for we believe that our multinational association can expand human understanding and understanding among nations, assist in the elimination of discrimination based on differences of race, colour or creed, maintain and strengthen personal liberty, contribute to the enrichment of life for all, and provide a powerful influence for peace among nations.

Singapore, 22 January 1971

APPENDIX III

LUSAKA DECLARATION OF THE COMMONWEALTH ON RACISM AND RACIAL PREJUDICE

LUSAKA DECLARATION OF THE COMMONWEALTH ON RACISM AND RACIAL PREJUDICE

We, Commonwealth Heads of Government, recalling the Declaration of Commonwealth Principles made at Singapore on 22 January 1971 and the statement on Apartheid in Sport, issued in London on 15 June 1977, have decided to proclaim our desire to work jointly as well as severally for the eradication of all forms of racism and racial prejudice.

The Commonwealth is an institution devoted to the promotion of international understanding and world peace, and to the achievement of equal rights for all citizens regardless of race, colour, sex, creed or political belief, and is committed to the eradication of the dangerous evils of racism and racial prejudice.

We now, therefore, proclaim this Lusaka Declaration of the Commonwealth on Racism and Racial Prejudice.

United in our desire to rid the world of the evils of racism and racial prejudice, we proclaim our faith in the inherent dignity and worth of the human person and declare that:

- the peoples of the Commonwealth have the right to live freely in dignity and equality, without any distinction or exclusion based on race, colour, sex, descent, or national or ethnic origin;
- while everyone is free to retain diversity in his or her culture and lifestyle, this diversity does not justify the perpetuation of racial prejudice or racial discriminatory practices;
- everyone has the right to equality before the law and equal justice under the law;
- everyone has the right to effective remedies and protection against any form of discrimination based on the grounds of race, colour, sex, descent, or national or ethnic origin.

We reject as inhuman and intolerable all policies designed to perpetuate apartheid, racial segregation or other policies based on theories that racial groups are or may be inherently superior or inferior.

We reaffirm that it is the duty of all the peoples of the Commonwealth to work together for the total eradication of the infamous policy of apartheid which is internationally recognised as a crime against the conscience and dignity of mankind and the very existence of which is an affront to humanity.

We agree that everyone has the right to protection against acts of incitement to racial hatred and discrimination, whether committed by individuals, groups or other organizations.

We affirm that there should be no discrimination based on race, colour, sex, descent or national or ethnic origin in the acquisition or exercise of the right to vote; in the field of civil rights or access to citizenship; or in the economic, social or cultural fields, particular education, health, employment, occupation, housing, social security and cultural life.

We attach particular importance to ensuring that children shall be protected from practices which may foster racism or racial prejudice. Children have the right to be brought up and educated in a spirit of tolerance and understanding so as to be able to contribute fully to the building of future societies based on justice and friendship.

We believe that those groups in societies who may be especially disadvantages because of residual racist attitudes are entitled to the fullest protection of the law.

We recognise that the history of the Commonwealth and its diversity require that special attention should be paid to the problems of indigenous minorities. We recognise that the same special attention should be paid to the problems of immigrants, immigrant workers and refugees.

We agree that special measures may in particular circumstances be required to advance the development of disadvantaged groups in society. We recognise that the effects of colonialism or racism in the past may make desirable special provisions for the social and economic enhancement of indigenous populations.

Inspired by the principles of freedom and equality which characterise our association, we accept the solemn duty of working together to eliminate racism and racial prejudice. This duty involves the acceptance of the principle that positive measures may be required to advance the elimination of racism, including assistance to those struggling to rid themselves and their environment of the practice.

Being aware that legislation alone cannot eliminate racism and racial prejudice, we endorse the need to initiate public information and education policies designed to promote understanding, tolerance, respect and friendship among peoples and racial groups.

We are particularly conscious of the importance of the contribution the media can make to human rights and the eradication of racism and racial prejudice by helping to eliminate ignorance and misunderstanding between people and by drawing attention to the evils which afflict humanity. We affirm the importance of truthful presentation of facts in order to ensure that the public are fully informed of the dangers presented by racism and racial prejudice.

In accordance with established principles of International Law and, in particular, the provisions of the International Convention on the Elimination of all Forms of Racial Discrimination, we affirm that everyone is, at all times and in all places, entitled to be protected in the enjoyment of the right to be free of racism and racial prejudice.

We believe that the existence in the world of apartheid and racial discrimination is a matter of concern to all human beings.We recognise that we share an international responsibility to work together for the total eradication of apartheid and racial discrimination.

We note that racism and racial prejudice, wherever they occur, are significant factors contributing to tension between nations and thus inhibit peaceful progress and development. We believe that the goal of the eradication of racism stands as a critical priority for governments of the Commonwealth, committed as they are to the promotion of the ideals of peaceful and happy lives for their people.

We intend that the Commonwealth, as an international organization with a fundamental and deep-rooted attachment to principles of freedom and equality, should co-operate with other organizations in the fulfilment of these principles. In particular the Commonwealth should seek to enhance the co-ordination of its activities with those of other organizations similarly committed to the promotion and protection of human rights and fundamental freedoms.

Lusaka, Zambia, 7 August 1979

APPENDIX IV

COMMONWEALTH HARARE DECLARATION, 1991

COMMONWEALTH HARARE DECLARATION, 1991

The Harare Declaration is the Commonwealth's second general statement of beliefs. It was issued by Commonwealth Heads of Government at their meeting in Zimbabwe in 1991. This Declaration, issued 20 years after the Declaration of Commonwealth Principles, reinforces the earlier declaration, updates it where necessary, and defines the core values to take the Commonwealth into the 21st century and beyond.

It also outlines a programme of action, placing priority on areas where the Commonwealth is particularly well placed to operate – such as in strengthening democracy, human rights and the rights of women.

The Heads of Government of the countries of the Commonwealth, meeting in Harare, reaffirm their confidence in the Commonwealth as a voluntary association of sovereign independent States, each responsible for its own policies, consulting and co-operating in the interests of their peoples and in the promotion of international understanding and world peace.

Members of the Commonwealth include people of many different races and origins, encompass every state of economic development, and comprise a rich variety of cultures, traditions and institutions.

The special strength of the Commonwealth lies in the combination of the diversity of its members with their shared inheritance in language, culture and the rule of law. The Commonwealth way is to seek consensus through consultation and the sharing of experience. It is uniquely placed to serve as a model and as a catalyst for new forms of friendship and co-operation to all in the spirit of the Charter of the United Nations.

Its members also share a commitment to certain fundamental principles. These were set out in a Declaration of Commonwealth Principles agreed by our predecessors at their Meeting in Singapore in 1971. Those principles have stood the test of time, and we reaffirm our full and continuing commitment to them today.

In particular, no less today than 20 years ago:

- we believe that international peace and order, global economic development and the rule of international law are essential to the security and prosperity of mankind;
- we believe in the liberty of the individual under the law, in equal rights for all citizens regardless of gender, race, colour, creed or political belief, and in the individual's inalienable right to participate by means of free and democratic political processes in framing the society in which he or she lives;

- we recognise racial prejudice and intolerance as a dangerous sickness and a threat to healthy development, and racial discrimination as an unmitigated evil;
- we oppose all forms of racial oppression, and we are committed to the principles of human dignity and equality;
- we recognise the importance and urgency of economic and social development to satisfy the basic needs and aspirations of the vast majority of the peoples of the world, and seek the progressive removal of the wide disparities in living standards amongst our members.

In Harare, our purpose has been to apply those principles in the contemporary situation as the Commonwealth prepares to face the challenges of the 1990s and beyond.

Internationally, the world is no longer locked in the iron grip of the Cold War. Totalitarianism is giving way to democracy and justice in many parts of the world. Decolonisation is largely complete. Significant changes are at last under way in South Africa. These changes, so desirable and heartening in themselves, present the world and the Commonwealth with new tasks and challenges.

In the last 20 years, several Commonwealth countries have made significant progress in economic and social development.

There is increasing recognition that commitment to market principles and openness to international trade and investment can promote economic progress and improve living standards. Many Commonwealth countries are poor and face acute problems, including excessive population growth, crushing poverty, debt burdens and environmental degradation. More than half our member states are particularly vulnerable because of their very small societies.

Only sound and sustainable development can offer these millions the prospect of betterment. Achieving this will require a flow of public and private resources from the developed to the developing world, and domestic and international regimes conducive to the realisation of these goals. Development facilitates the task of tackling a range of problems which affect the whole global community such as environmental degradation, the problems of migration and refugees, the fight against communicable diseases, and drug production and trafficking.

Having reaffirmed the principles to which the Commonwealth is committed, and reviewed the problems and challenges which the world, and the Commonwealth as part of it, face, we pledge the Commonwealth and our countries to work with renewed vigour, concentrating especially in the following areas:

- the protection and promotion of the fundamental political values of the Commonwealth:
    - democracy, democratic processes and institutions which reflect national circumstances, the rule of law and the independence of the judiciary, just and honest government;
    - fundamental human rights, including equal rights and opportunities for all citizens regardless of race, colour, creed or political belief;
- equality for women, so that they may exercise their full and equal rights;
- provision of universal access to education for the population of our countries;
- continuing action to bring about the end of apartheid and the establishment of a free, democratic, non-racial and prosperous South Africa;
- the promotion of sustainable development and the alleviation of poverty in the countries of the Commonwealth through:
    - a stable international economic framework within which growth can be achieved;
    - sound economic management recognising the central role of the market economy;
    - effective population policies and programmes;
    - sound management of technological change;
    - the freest possible flow of multilateral trade on terms fair and equitable to all, taking account of the special requirements of developing countries;
    - an adequate flow of resources from the developed to developing countries, and action to alleviate the debt burdens of developing countries most in need;
    - the development of human resources, in particular through education, training, health, culture, sport and programmes for strengthening family and community support, paying special attention to the needs of women, youth and children;
    - effective and increasing programmes of bilateral and multilateral co-operation aimed at raising living standards;
- extending the benefits of development within a framework of respect for human rights;
- the protection of the environment through respect for the principles of sustainable development which we enunciated at Langkawi;
- action to combat drug trafficking and abuse and communicable diseases;

- help for small Commonwealth States in tackling their particular economic and security problems;

- support of the United Nations and other international institutions in the world's search for peace, disarmament and effective arms control; and in the promotion of international consensus on major global political, economic and social issues.

To give weight and effectiveness to our commitments, we intend to focus and improve Commonwealth co-operation in these areas. This would include strengthening the capacity of the Commonwealth to respond to requests from members for assistance in entrenching the practices of democracy, accountable administration and the rule of law.

We call on all the intergovernmental institutions of the Commonwealth to seize the opportunities presented by these challenges. We pledge ourselves to assist them to develop programmes which harness our shared historical, professional, cultural and linguistic heritage and which complement the work of other international and regional organizations.

We invite the Commonwealth Parliamentary Association and non-governmental Commonwealth organizations to play their full part in promoting these objectives, in a spirit of co-operation and mutual support.

In reaffirming the principles of the Commonwealth and in committing ourselves to pursue them in policy and action in response to the challenges of the 1990s, in areas where we believe that the Commonwealth has a distinctive contribution to offer, we the Heads of Government express our determination to renew and enhance the value and importance of the Commonwealth as an institution which can and should strengthen and enrich the lives not only of its own members and their peoples but also of the wider community of peoples of which they are a part.

Harare, Zimbabwe, 20 October 1991

APPENDIX V

THE MILLBROOK COMMONWEALTH ACTION PROGRAMME ON THE HARARE DECLARATION, 1995

THE MILLBROOK COMMONWEALTH ACTION PROGRAMME ON THE HARARE DECLARATION, 1995

At Harare in 1991, we pledged to work for the protection and promotion of the fundamental political values of the association, namely democracy, democratic processes and institutions which reflect national circumstances, fundamental human rights, the rule of law and the independence of the judiciary, and just and honest government. We agreed at the same time to work for the promotion of socio-economic development, recognising its high priority for most Commonwealth countries. During our Retreat at Millbrook, we decided to adopt a Commonwealth Action Programme to fulfil more effectively the commitments contained in the Harare Commonwealth Declaration. This Programme is in three parts:

I   advancing Commonwealth fundamental political values;

II   promoting sustainable development; and

III facilitating consensus building.

I   Advancing Commonwealth fundamental political values

A   *Measures in Support of Processes and Institutions for the Practice of the Harare Principles*

The Secretariat should enhance its capacity to provide advice, training and other forms of technical assistance to governments in promoting the Commonwealth's fundamental political values, including:

- assistance in creating and building the capacity of requisite institutions;
- assistance in constitutional and legal matters, including with selecting models and initiating programmes of democratisation;
- assistance in the electoral field, including the establishment or strengthening of independent electoral machinery, civic and voter education, the preparation of Codes of Conduct, and assistance with voter registration;
- observation of elections, including by-elections or local elections where appropriate, at the request of the member governments concerned;
- strengthening the rule of law and promoting the independence of the judiciary through the promotion of exchanges among, and training of, the judiciary;

- support for good government, particularly in the area of public service reform; and

- other activities, in collaboration with the Commonwealth Parliamentary Association and other bodies, to strengthen the democratic culture and effective parliamentary practices.

B   *Measures in Response to Violations of the Harare Principles*

Where a member country is perceived to be clearly in violation of the Harare Commonwealth Declaration, and particularly in the event of an unconstitutional overthrow of a democratically elected government, appropriate steps should be taken to express the collective concern of Commonwealth countries and to encourage the restoration of democracy within a reasonable time frame. These include:

i   immediate public expression by the Secretary General of the Commonwealth's collective disapproval of any such infringement of the Harare principles;

ii   early contact by the Secretary General with the de facto government, followed by continued good offices and appropriate technical assistance to facilitate an early restoration of democracy;

iii encouraging bilateral démarches by member countries, especially those within the region, both to express disapproval and to support early restoration of democracy;

iv   appointment of an envoy or a group of eminent Commonwealth representatives where, following the Secretary General's contacts with the authorities concerned, such a mission is deemed beneficial in reinforcing the Commonwealth's good offices role;

v   stipulation of up to two years as the time frame for the restoration of democracy where the institutions are not in place to permit the holding of elections within, say, a maximum of six months;

vi   pending restoration of democracy, exclusion of the government concerned from participation at ministerial level meetings of the Commonwealth, including CHOGMs;

vii suspension of participation at all Commonwealth meetings and of Commonwealth technical assistance if acceptable progress is not recorded by the government concerned after a period of two years; and

viii consideration of appropriate further bilateral and multilateral measures by all member States (for example, limitation of government to government contacts; people to people measures; trade restrictions; and, in exceptional cases, suspension from the association), to reinforce the need for change in the event that the government concerned chooses to leave the Commonwealth and/or persists in violating the principles of the Harare Commonwealth Declaration even after two years.

C *Mechanism for implementation of measures*

We have decided to establish a Commonwealth Ministerial Action Group on the Harare Declaration in order to deal with serious or persistent violations of the principles contained in that Declaration. The Group will be convened by the Secretary General and will comprise the Foreign Ministers of eight countries, supplemented as appropriate by one or two additional ministerial representatives from the region concerned. It will be the Group's task to assess the nature of the infringement and recommend measures for collective Commonwealth action aimed at the speedy restoration of democracy and constitutional rule.

The composition, terms of reference and operation of the Group will be reviewed by us every two years.

II Promoting sustainable development

We reaffirmed our view that the Commonwealth should continue to be a source of help in promoting development and literacy and in eradicating poverty, particularly as these bear on women and children. With a view to enhancing its capacity in this area, we agreed on the following steps:

i to strengthen the Secretariat's capacity for undertaking developmental work through support for its various funds and especially by restoring the resources of the CFTC to their 1991/92 level in real terms; and to provide adequate resources to the Commonwealth of Learning and to the Commonwealth Foundation;

ii to support a greater flow of investment to developing member countries through such schemes as the Commonwealth Private Investment Initiative;

iii to work for continued progress in assisting countries with unsustainable debt burdens and to promote enhanced multilateral concessional financial flows to developing countries; in particular, to support new and innovative mechanisms for relief on multilateral debt, such as the one proposed by the British Chancellor of the Exchequer at the 1994 Commonwealth Finance Ministers Meeting in Malta, and reiterated subsequently;

iv to support the Secretariat in facilitating the adoption by more Commonwealth countries of successful self-help schemes, with non-governmental agencies and others acting as catalytic agents, for mobilising the energies of people in alleviating poverty;

v to support the efforts of small island developing States to mitigate the effects on their development of environmental change, natural disasters and the changing international trading system; and

vi to combat the spread of HIV/AIDS, which threatens large parts of the younger population of many countries, recognising that the effective exploitation of economic opportunities requires a healthy and educated population; and to provide further resources to renew the core funding of the Southern African Network of AIDS Organizations (SANASO), along with increased funding for UNICEF initiatives in Southern Africa.

III Facilitating consensus building

We were convinced that the Commonwealth, with its global reach and unique experience of consensus building, was in a position to assist the wider international community in building bridges across traditional international divides of opinion on particular issues. We therefore agreed that there was scope for the association to play a greater role in the search for consensus on global issues, through:

i use of their governments membership of various regional organizations and attendance at other international gatherings to advance consensual positions agreed within the Commonwealth;

ii use, where appropriate, of special missions to advance Commonwealth consensual positions and promote wider consensus on issues of major international concern; and

iii use of formal and informal Commonwealth consultations in the wings of meetings of international institutions with a view to achieving consensus on major concerns.

Heads of Government, Millbrook, New Zealand

12 November 1995

APPENDIX VI

COMMONWEALTH LAW MINISTERS' STATEMENT ON PREVENTION OF CORRUPTION

COMMONWEALTH LAW MINISTERS' STATEMENT ON PREVENTION OF CORRUPTION

Commonwealth Law Ministers, meeting in Kuala Lumpur from 15 to 19 April 1996, acknowledged the existence of corruption in the provision of services in the public interest, whether by the public or the private sector, as a serious multi-dimensional national and international problem which inhibits development, creates poverty, destroys confidence in the legal and political systems, and undermines good governance.

Ministers recognised the threat posed by corruption to democratic institutions and good governance, and the need to combat corruption effectively in order to achieve the goals set out in the Harare Declaration, as elaborated upon by the Millbrook Commonwealth Action Programme.

They therefore considered it essential that those holding leadership positions demonstrate by their personal conduct their commitment to integrity and that they support all those responsible for preventing and combating corruption. Further, they emphasised that measures which nurture the evolution of a democratic society – characterised by an independent judiciary, open government operating by way of transparent procedures, democratically constituted institutions, an adequately remunerated public service, and free and responsible mass media – should be protected and encouraged. In this context, ministers noted various structural devices that had been employed by a number of member countries, such as financial accountability requirements, anti-corruption commissions, freedom of information legislation and public accounts committees.

In terms of the economic effects of corruption, it was noted that corruption in international business transactions and foreign aid projects can contribute to the initiation of unnecessary projects and to the diversion of funds and resources from projects which are vitally necessary. Ministers expressed approval of the work of the OECD in addressing the fact that bribes paid by foreign businesses, particularly from industrialised countries and which are often tax deductible in their home countries, are conducive to the creation of corrupt cultures.

Ministers also noted that there is a growing need for the network of mechanisms for combating corruption to cover the provision of services in the public interest by the private sector, given the trends towards contracting out and the privatisation of services previously provided by government entities and the shift in the nature of governance which this entails.

The links that often exist between corruption, drug trafficking, and organized crime were recognised and the need for continuing and improved mutual legal assistance in investigations and prosecutions in relation to criminal offences emphasised.

Ministers noted the diversity of national laws and experiences of Commonwealth jurisdictions in the field of preventing and combatting corruption and stressed the need to share knowledge of these. They were encouraged by those strategies which have achieved some success, and identified the need for an 'holistic' approach which combines a number of strategies rather than pursuing any of them in isolation. Key strategies to be applied in combination should include a political commitment to the eradication of corruption, effective anti-corruption legislation, and adequate remuneration of public officials. They recognised, however, that none of these strategies would succeed without the creation of a culture hostile to corruption and that in this regard public education has an important role to play.

The initiatives of other international bodies such as the International Anti-Corruption Conferences and the OECD were also noted with interest. Ministers emphasised the need for the Commonwealth to co-ordinate and liaise with them.

Ministers therefore express their collective commitment to work on both the domestic and international fronts to combat corruption. In particular, they:

1   Undertake to implement strategies to prevent and combat corruption, to the extent that they have not already done so, and to keep the Secretariat fully informed of relevant developments.

2   Call upon the Secretariat, in consultation with member governments, to examine all aspects of the problem, to advise ministers on developments and initiatives in the field, to propose courses of action which may assist member jurisdictions to address and to resolve the problems of corruption more effectively, and in particular to:

(a) collect and disseminate examples of national laws and experiences in combatting corruption, and advise on developments and initiatives in the international field;

(b) identify those strategies which have been effective in changing national and international standards, especially those strategies which have helped to promote an 'anti-corruption' culture; and

(c) develop model legal strategies for combating corruption, including an appropriate legal framework which takes into account the increasing role of the private sector in the system of government. This will include the development of minimum standards for Commonwealth members in the form of a Model Integrity Code.

3   Request the Secretariat to co-operate with other intergovernmental; and non-governmental organizations working to combat corruption.

4   Commit themselves to ensure that national responses to Commonwealth initiatives on mutual assistance in criminal matters and the rendition of fugitive offenders are fully applicable to corruption offences.

5   Agree to establish an advisory working group which shall be convened by the Secretariat and which shall advise and assist the Secretariat in the performance of its tasks.

APPENDIX VII

INTERNATIONAL INSTRUMENTS
AFFECTING WOMEN'S RIGHTS

INTERNATIONAL INSTRUMENTS AFFECTING WOMEN'S RIGHTS

- Declaration on the Elimination of Violence Against Women (1993)

- Convention on the Elimination of Discrimination Against Women (1979)

- Declaration on the Protection of Women and Children in Emergencies and Armed Conflicts (1974)

- Declaration on the Elimination of Discrimination Against Women (1967)

- Convention on Consent to Marriage, Minimum Age for Marriage and Registration of Marriages (1962)

- Convention Against Discrimination in Education (Adopted by the General Conference of UNESCO, 14 December 1960)

- Discrimination (Employment and Occupation) Convention (1958)

- Convention on the Political Rights of Women (1952)

- ILO Equal Remuneration Convention (1951)

- Convention for the Suppression of the Traffic in Persons and of the Exploitation of the Prostitution of Others (1949)